HOME ECONOMICS

Standard Grade COURSE NOTES

Alastair MacGregor

Published by
Leckie & Leckie Ltd, 8 Whitehill Terrace, St Andrews, Scotland KY16 8RN
tel: 01334 475656 fax: 01334 477392
hq@leckieandleckie.co.uk www.leckieandleckie.co.uk

Edited by Margaret Wilson

Special thanks to
Simon Appleford (page make up), Exodus-AD (design), Mike Middleton (cover design), David Nicoll (project management) and Finola Stack (illustration)

ISBN 1-84372-034-5

A CIP Catalogue record for this book is available from the British Library.

Printed in Scotland by Inglis Allen on environmentally friendly paper. The paper is made from a mixture of sawmill waste, forest thinnings and wood from sustainable forests.

® Leckie & Leckie is a registered trademark.

2nd edition

Leckie & Leckie

Leckie & Leckie has made every effort to trace all copyright holders. If any have been inadvertently overlooked, Leckie & Leckie will be pleased to make the necessary arrangements. Leckie & Leckie would like to thank the following for their permission to reproduce their material:

The Soil Association for the Organic Standard logo (p 93);
The Vegan Society for the Vegan Society trademark (p 93);
The British Toy & Hobby Association for the Lion Mark logo (p 94);
Kitemark reproduced with the permission of BSI under licence number 2002SK/0113 (p 95);
The British Electrotechnical Approvals Board for the BEAB Approved logo (p 95);
The European Union Eco-Labelling Board for the EU Flower logo (p 95);
The Council for Registered Gas Installers for the CORGI logo (p 95).

Introduction

Home Economics is an unfortunate title for a course that has such an impact on your life and the life of others. It suggests something a bit dry and old-fashioned. Whereas the reality of this course is founded in contemporary, bang up-to-date thinking, giving you the necessary information to enable you to build the foundations of a healthy and fulfilling life.

It's no secret that we Scots have a history of poor diet and appalling health statistics. We need to change this. We live in a country surrounded by an embarrassment of riches, some of the best foods to be found anywhere in the world, and easy access to open, unpolluted countryside offering every conceivable leisure pursuit. And do we take advantage of this? Unfortunately the statistics say no. It's a matter of personal regret to me that I didn't discover the benefits of a healthy lifestyle until I was in my 30s. This course offers you all the information you need to live well and get the best out of your life – I suggest you start right now and make healthy living a habit for life!

These Course Notes contain everything you need to know, laid out in an easy-to-read, entertaining format fully explaining where you should target your endeavours. I really wish I had had this information when I was at school. You want a healthy lifestyle to be a source of satisfaction, not regret. You only have one life – make it a good one!

Nick Nairn

Nick Nairn teaches at his own first class school. Visit www.nairnscookschool.com and read all about it!

Knowledge and Understanding

Eating a variety of foods contributes to health

Main nutrients, their sources and functions

Relationship between water, non-starch polysaccharides and health

Health and nutrient intake

Interrelationship of nutrients ➜

The main nutrients, their sources and functions

There will always be questions in the exam paper about nutrients. The chart below details all the information that you will need to know in the examination. The highlighted information is required only by candidates who will sit a credit examination.

Credit Only

Nutrition is the study of food and how the body uses it.
Nutrients are chemicals that are found in food. The body needs nutrients if it is to work properly.

Nutrient	Food Sources	Functions in the body
Protein	Animal sources: meat, fish, milk, cheese and eggs Vegetable sources: peas, beans, nuts, lentils and cereals	Required for the growth, repair and maintenance of body tissues Any excess protein can be broken down and used as a source of energy

Credit Only

Protein is made up of amino acids. There are over 20 different amino acids. Adults require eight of these amino acids for growth, repair and maintenance. Children require ten. Animal sources contain all ten essential amino acids and are called High Biological Value (HBV) proteins. Plant sources do not contain all the ten essential amino acids and are called Low Biological Value (LBV) proteins. Soya bean is a vegetable source of protein but contains all ten essential amino acids.

Nutrient	Food Sources	Functions in the body
Carbohydrate: Sugar and starch	Cereals and cereal foods, vegetables, fruits, milk, refined sugar and products containing refined sugar (e.g. cakes and biscuits, jams, soft drinks)	A major source of energy Excess carbohydrate that is not used for energy can be converted into body fat and so can provide warmth.

Credit Only

Carbohydrates can be subdivided into three main groups:
Monosaccharides: *glucose* (naturally found in fruit and plant juices), *fructose* (naturally found in some fruits and vegetables, as well as honey) and *galactose* (produced as a result of the digestive process).
Disaccharides: *sucrose* (naturally found in sugar cane and beet and in some vegetables e.g. carrots); *maltose* (formed during digestion and in the fermentation of grain); *lactose* (found only in milk).
Polysaccharides: *starch* is a polysaccharide found in bread, flour, potatoes and cakes. *Non-starch polysaccharides* (NSP) are a form of polysaccharides. See later sections for more information.

Nutrient	Food Sources	Functions in the body
Fat	Animal sources: butter, lard, cream, meat, oily fish, milk, cheese and many baked foods Vegetable sources: olive oil, margarine, nuts and some salad dressings	A concentrated source of energy to the body Warmth – excess fat is stored under the skin providing an insulating layer. Provides essential fatty acids Provides an adequate source of fat-soluble vitamins A, D, E and K

Credit Only

Fats can be classified as either saturated or unsaturated. Saturated fats are mainly from animal sources and are considered to be bad for health. Unsaturated fats are considered to be better for the body. Unsaturated fats can be further divided into monounsaturated fats (e.g. olive oil and fish oils) and polyunsaturated fats (e.g. polyunsaturated margarine).

Essential fatty acids are found in vegetable oils and must be obtained directly from foods as the body cannot manufacture them. This is one reason why we are encouraged to consume unsaturated rather than saturated fats.

Vitamins

Vitamins are essential to general health. Each vitamin is required in only relatively small quantities and each has a particular function in the body. Vitamins are classified according to whether they are soluble in fat or in water.

Fat soluble vitamins

Nutrient	Food Sources	Functions in the body
Vitamin A (Retinol)	Animal sources: liver, butter, cheese, margarine, sardines, meat, eggs, cheese and fish liver oils.	Required for growth in children Assists with good vision – particularly vision in dim light Protects surface tissues (e.g. linings of the nose, mouth, throat and eyes)
(Carotene)	Plant sources: spinach, carrots and green vegetables.	

Carotene is converted into Vitamin A in the small intestine. Six units of Carotene are equal to one unit of Retinol.

Nutrient	Food Sources	Functions in the body
Vitamin D	Sunlight, fish liver oils, oily fish, egg yolk, liver, margarine, fortified breakfast cereals	Essential with calcium and phosphorus for the development of strong bones and teeth Promotes quicker healing of bone fractures Allows calcium to be absorbed in the small intestine

The action of sunlight on the skin results in the formation of vitamin D in the body. People who do not get out into the sunshine (e.g. the housebound, invalids) may suffer from a deficiency.

Credit Only

Nutrient	Food Sources	Functions in the body
Vitamin E	Vegetable oils, eggs, liver and meat, wheat germ, oatmeal, margarine. Leafy green vegetables contain a small amount.	Classed as one of the anti-oxidant vitamins as it is thought to have a link in the prevention of certain cancers Involved in the maintenance of cell membranes

Credit Only

Nutrient	Food Sources	Function in the body
Vitamin K	Leafy green vegetables, eggs, milk	Required for the clotting of blood (New-born babies are given a vitamin K injection at birth.)

Water soluble vitamins

Nutrient	Food Sources	Functions in the body
Vitamin C	Mainly in fruits and vegetables: peppers, blackcurrants, cabbage, strawberries, citrus fruit, green vegetables, potatoes	Helps in the formation of connective tissue and in the absorption of iron Helps prevent infections Essential in the formation of the walls of blood vessels

Water soluble vitamins (continued)

Nutrient	Food Sources	Functions in the body
Vitamin B1 (thiamin)	Milk, flour, bread, fortified breakfast cereals, meat, cereals, brown rice, liver, kidney, eggs	Release of energy from carbohydrates Growth and functioning of nervous system Maintains muscle tone

Nutrient	Food Sources	Functions in the body
Vitamin B2 (riboflavin)	Milk, eggs, green vegetables, yeast, liver, kidney, meat. Some is also manufactured in the intestines.	Release of energy from protein, carbohydrates and fat Required for normal growth in children

Nutrient	Food Sources	Functions in the body
Folic Acid	Liver, kidneys, dark leafy vegetables, whole grain cereals, whole-wheat bread, pulses	Required in the formation of red blood cells Has a role in the prevention of neural tube defects (e.g. spina bifida) in developing foetuses

Antioxidant vitamins

Credit Only

Vitamins A, C and E are sometimes referred to as antioxidant vitamins. A diet rich in antioxidant vitamins is thought to help reduce the risk of heart disease and cancers.

Research indicates that sufficient intake of vitamin C offers vital protection against cancer. Studies also indicate that the higher the level of vitamins A and C, the lower the risk of heart disease.

Minerals

Like vitamins, minerals are essential to general health. Each one is required in only relatively small quantities, but each has particular functions in the body.

Nutrient	Food Sources	Function in the body
Iron	Red meat – particularly offal (kidneys, liver), bread, flour, cereal products, green leafy vegetables.	Required for red blood cell formation. Red blood cells assist in the movement of oxygen around the body.

Iron is required for the formation of a substance in the blood called haemoglobin. This is the substance that red blood cells use to transport oxygen from the lungs to body tissues.

Minerals (continued)

Nutrient	Food Sources	Functions in the body
Calcium	Milk, cheese, yoghurt, flour, bread, green vegetables, canned fish	Growth and development of bones and teeth Required for the normal clotting of blood Also required for the normal functioning of nerves and muscles

The material that gives teeth and bones their hardness is calcium phosphate, which is made from the minerals calcium and phosphorus. Although both are required for strong bones and teeth, they also have important independent functions in the body.

Nutrient	Food Sources	Functions in the body
Fluoride	Often found dissolved in drinking water if the water supply has been fluoridated. It is also found in small quantities in tea and sea water fish.	Fluoride is essential for hardening the enamel of teeth. It has a role in ensuring that bones have the correct amounts of minerals deposited in them.

Fluoride is often found in commercial toothpastes. Excessive fluoride in the diet can lead to the mottling of teeth.

Nutrient	Food Sources	Functions in the body
Sodium	Salt, bacon, cheese, some savoury snack products such as crisps	Required to maintain the correct concentration of body fluids Also required for correct muscle and nerve activity

Credit Only

Nutrient	Food Sources	Functions in the body
Phosphorus	Found in most foods, especially milk, milk products, cereal products, meat and meat products, nuts.	Works in conjunction with calcium to give strength to bones and teeth Phosphorus is a component of all cells and is required so that the body can obtain energy from foods.

Most foods rich in calcium are also rich in phosphorus, but not vice versa.

Generally, all examination papers will ask a question about the sources and functions of at least one of the major nutrients listed above. You would not normally be asked to give more than two functions of a particular nutrient. It is important that you know the main food sources of a nutrient, because a question might ask you to identify nutrients found in a specific meal or food.

Relationship between water, non-starch polysaccharides and health

Water

Water is not a nutrient but it is essential for life. The human body is about 65% water.

Food Sources	Functions in the body
Most foods contain water. Fruits and vegetables consist mainly of water. Water is supplied in the diet as drinking water as well as in liquid products such as milk.	• Water is vital to life. • Required for all body fluids (e.g. blood, saliva, sweat, urine) • Helps in the removal of waste products from body tissues and organs • Some nutrients are dissolved in water for better absorption. • Lubricates joints and mucous membranes

Water should be consumed daily. During exercise and in hot weather we sweat. This means that our bodies lose water that needs to be replaced. Sweating cools the body as perspiration evaporates from the surface of the skin. Water is lost daily through sweat, urine, faeces and breathing.

Extra water may be required during illness; when a raised temperature may increase sweating; when vomiting or diarrhoea has occurred, both of which can cause rapid dehydration (especially in small children); and during lactation when milk is being produced to breastfeed babies.

Non-starch polysaccharide (NSP)

NSP provides the firm and fibrous structure of fruits, vegetables and cereal products. This part of the food is the part that cannot be digested by the body. For this reason, NSP is not classed as a nutrient.

Food Sources	Functions in the body
Wholegrain cereals (e.g. oats, wheat, rice, wholemeal bread). Fruits (especially in the skins) and vegetables, especially potato skins and leafy vegetables.	• NSP absorbs water and binds other food residues to itself, so making the faeces soft and bulky and easy to remove from the body. • NSP helps to 'mop up' any poisonous toxins found in waste products. • NSP gives a feeling of fullness and so may be useful as part of a calorie controlled diet. This is due to the fact that an NSP-rich diet will slow down the digestive process and so we feel 'fuller' for a longer period of time. • Consumption of NSP has been associated with reductions in cholesterol. • A diet rich in NSP can prevent constipation, bowel diseases (such as cancer of the colon) and diverticular disease.

Health and nutrient intake

The following terms are often used when talking about nutrition:

Balanced diet – this is a diet in which the correct amounts of nutrients are available for the needs of a person.
Under nutrition – there is an insufficient total intake of nutrients to allow the body to function correctly.
Malnutrition – there is an unbalanced or incorrect intake of nutrients.
Metabolism – this is a series of chemical reactions that takes place within the body and enables the body to function correctly.

The relationship between health and energy

Energy is not a nutrient. When your body digests nutrients (fat, carbohydrate and protein), energy is released, allowing your body to carry out all its functions and activities. It is important that the amount of energy supplied by your food equals the amount of energy you require for your body to carry out all its functions and activities. If you do not consume enough energy-providing foods, you may become tired and listless – you are 'lacking in energy'. If you take in too much energy from the food you eat and your body cannot use it all, it is stored as fat. It is important that you get this energy balance right. The body must have energy so if you are not consuming sufficient energy-rich foods, your body may use protein for its source of energy. This means that you may become deficient in protein.

The relationship between health and protein

We have seen already that protein is essential to life, but what happens when the protein balance is not right? If you take in too much protein, the excess is converted to fat and stored in your body. This can lead to a person becoming overweight. If you do not consume enough protein-rich foods, your body cannot carry out its normal functions of growth and repair. On page 11 we looked at HBV and LBV protein foods. HBV protein foods contain all eight essential amino acids required for growth and repair. LBV protein foods are missing at least one of these essential amino acids. These foods can compensate for each other's deficiencies if eaten together and in sufficient quantities. A good example is beans and wholemeal toast. The amino acids that are missing in beans are found in the toast and vice versa, i.e. one food complements the other.

In many developing countries the traditional diet is based on cereals such as rice. The protein content of cereal products is generally of a low biological value, so the diets of people in these areas may be deficient in protein. By contrast, in developed countries there is generally an excess of protein in the diet, leading to storage of fat in the body.

The multi-nutrient value of food

Most foods contain more than one nutrient, and so are of use to the body in different ways. It is important that a balanced diet is eaten to ensure that a good balance of nutrients is consumed, as no single food provides the body with all the nutrients that it requires to function properly. Some foods, such as sugar, contain only one nutrient (in this case carbohydrate) and so are of more limited use to the body.

In your written examination you may be asked to identify the nutrients found in specific foods. This is why it is important that you have a good knowledge of nutrition.

Interrelationship of nutrients

Credit Only

Our body requires a large number of nutrients if it is to function well. Many nutrients have similar functions, indeed some nutrients work together for specific functions. In the Credit Level examination paper you may get asked a question about the interrelationships between different nutrients. When answering this type of question it is important that you do not just restate the function of each individual nutrient – this is not what the question is asking.

Calcium, phosphorus and vitamin D

These three nutrients commonly work together. Each has additional uses in the body, but they have an important role to play together.

The material which gives both bones and teeth their hardness is a substance called calcium phosphate. This is a process called calcification, where bones and teeth become enmeshed with calcium phosphate and become stronger. A supply of both calcium and phosphorous is required before this process can take place.

The amount of calcium that is available to the body is controlled by vitamin D. If there is insufficient vitamin D in the diet, less calcium will be available.

Iron and vitamin C

These two nutrients commonly work together. Each may have additional uses in the body, but they have an important role to play together.

Vitamin C has an important role to play in assisting with the absorption of iron. The body can readily absorb only about 10% of the iron that is present in food. The remainder must be changed into a form of iron that the body can easily absorb. Vitamin C helps in this process. For this reason it is important when planning meals to ensure that there is sufficient vitamin C rich food in the diet.

There are a variety of factors that assist in the absorption of nutrients and a variety of factors that hinder the absorption of nutrients.

- A good supply of vitamin D
- Protein
- Lactose (the sugar found in milk)

- A good supply of vitamin C

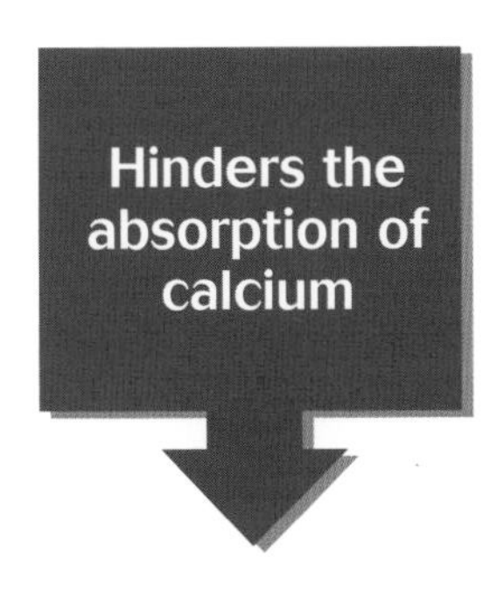

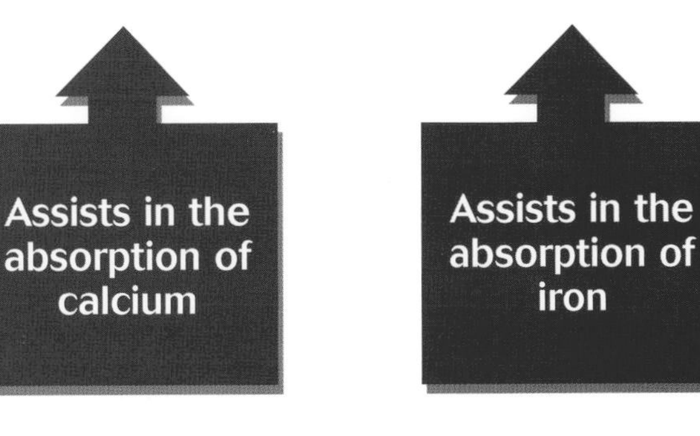

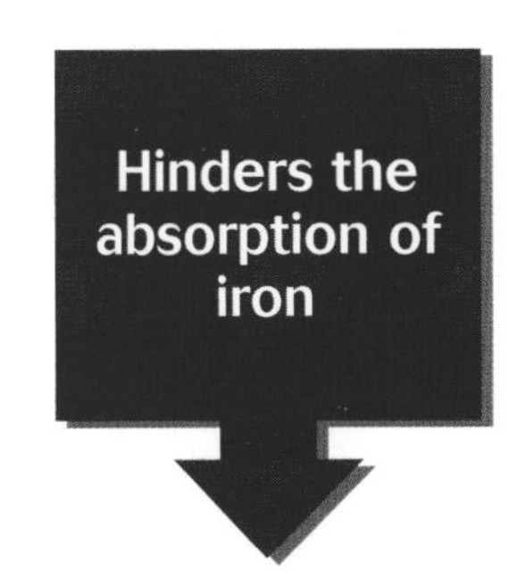

- A type of acid found in wholegrain cereal (Phytic acid)
- NSP
- Fats – particularly saturated
- A type of acid found in spinach (Oxalic acid)

- NSP
- A type of acid found in wholegrain cereal (Phytic acid)

Current dietary advice

Dietary targets

Ways to meet current dietary targets

Choice of cooking methods

Relationship between diet and health

Food labelling ➜

Dietary targets

There will always be questions to do with current dietary advice in the examination papers at Foundation, General and Credit levels. These questions are always based on the Scottish dietary targets. If you can remember all the targets listed below, they will stand you in good stead for your examination.

Dietary target linked to	Foundation level	General level	Credit level
Fruit and vegetables	Advised to eat more	Intake to double	Intake to double **to 400 grams per day.**
Bread	Advised to eat more	Intake to increase, mainly using wholemeal and brown bread	Intake to increase by **45% from present daily intake.**
Breakfast cereal	Advised to eat more	Intake to double	Intake to **double to 34 grams per day.**
Total complex carbohydrates (TCC)	Advised to eat more fruit and vegetables, bread, breakfast cereals, rice and pasta as well as potatoes	Intake to increase by a quarter through eating more fruit and vegetables, bread, breakfast cereals, rice and pasta as well as potatoes	Intake to increase **by 25%** through eating more fruit and vegetables, bread, breakfast cereals, rice and pasta. Potato consumption to increase **by 25%.**
Fish	Advised to eat more fish, especially oily fish	Intake of white fish to be maintained. Intake of oily fish to double.	Intake of white fish to be maintained. Intake of oily fish to double from **44 grams per week to 88 grams per week.**
Salt	Advised to eat less	Average intake to reduce	Average intake to reduce from **163 mmol per day to 100 mmol per day.**
Sugar	Adult intake not to increase Intake by children to reduce by half	Adult intake of Non Milk Extrinsic (NME) sugars not to rise Intake of NME sugars by children to reduce by half	Adult intake of NME sugars not to rise Intake of NME sugars by children to reduce by half **i.e. to less than 10% of energy.**
Fats	Advised to eat less fat, especially saturated fat	Average intake of total fat to be reduced Average intake of saturated fat to be reduced	Average intake of total fat to be reduced **to no more than 35% of food energy.** Average intake of saturated fat to be reduced **to no more than 11% of food energy.**

Items in **colour** – are not essential for Foundation or General levels. They are helpful to learn for Credit level.

There is a dietary target specific to breastfeeding. It is unlikely that you will be able to use this target when adapting meals for people. However there are sometimes questions linked to specific targets.

Dietary target linked to	Foundation level	General level	Credit level
Breastfeeding	More mothers should breastfeed their babies.	Breastfeeding should be encouraged in the first 6 weeks of a baby's life.	The proportion of mothers breastfeeding their babies in the first 6 weeks of life should increase **to more than 50%.**

Whilst it is important to know what the dietary targets are, it is just as important to know how to adapt food, and different preparation and cooking methods, to help meet the dietary targets.

Ways to meet current dietary targets

It is very unlikely that you would be asked to state more than four different ways of adapting foods or menus to meet current dietary targets. The tables below will help you with these types of questions.

Ways to increase vegetable content of the diet

A variety of salads and/or vegetables can be included with each meal.

Extra vegetables can be added to soups and stews.

Some vegetables can be used to make healthy drinks as alternatives to sugary fizzy drinks.

Some vegetables (e.g. carrots, cucumber, celery) can be eaten as snacks.

Ways to increase the fish content of the diet

Fish can be used to replace some meat in certain dishes (e.g. stir fry, fish burgers, risotto).

Oily fish can be used in a wide range of products (e.g. as a filling for pitta bread or pizza topping).

Fish can be used to make soups and some sauces.

Different types of fish can be used for a starter (e.g. prawn cocktail, mackerel pâté).

Ways to increase bread content of the diet

Wholemeal bread should begin to replace white bread (e.g. in sandwiches).

Bread can be used to make healthy puddings (e.g. bread pudding and summer fruit pudding).

Breadcrumbs for coating food can be made from wholemeal bread.

Breadcrumbs can be added to provide bulk to some foods (e.g. to homemade beef burgers).

Ways to increase breakfast cereal intake

Eat a bowl of wholegrain breakfast cereal in the morning or as a snack.

Use crushed wholegrain breakfast cereals as a topping for pies and desserts.

Add crushed breakfast cereals to biscuit or scone doughs.

Use crushed breakfast cereals as a coating for food to be baked or fried.

Ways to increase TCC content of the diet

Use rice or pasta instead of chips.

Home-made soups using grains and pulses can be used instead of packet soups.

Wholemeal flour can be substituted for white flour.

Wholegrain breakfast cereals should be used instead of sugar coated breakfast cereals.

Ways to increase fruit content of the diet

Fruit can be eaten as a snack.

Fruit-based puddings should be eaten rather than jam- or syrup-based puddings.

Fresh fruit juice can be used instead of sugary fizzy drinks.

Fruits can be added to many baked products (e.g. muffins).

Ways to reduce fat content of the diet

Choose lean cuts of meat or trim visible fat from meat.

Use low fat products (e.g. low fat cheese, yoghurt, and salad dressing) where possible.

Prevent adding additional fat to food (e.g. glazing vegetables with butter, extra fat added to cooking).

Fat should be skimmed from gravies, soups, stews and mince after cooking.

Ways to reduce the sugar content of the diet

Reduce the amount of sugar used in recipes for baking and puddings, use artificial sweetener instead, or add some dried fruit for sweetness.

Fruit tinned in natural juice is better than fruit tinned in syrup.

Low calorie/sugar free drinks and products should be used.

Eat fruit as a snack rather than sweets, cake or biscuits.

Ways to reduce salt intake in the diet

Reduce the amount of salt added during cooking/do not add salt at the table.

Use herbs and spices to season rather than salt.

Use stock cubes and soy sauce sparingly as they have added salt.

Use low salt products if available (there are salt alternatives available in supermarkets).

Alcohol is often used in cookery and is sometimes served along with meals. Alcohol provides a lot of energy and is associated with some health problems. The following measures should be followed to reduce the intake of alcohol:

- When cooking, substitute stock for wine or other alcohol.
- Alcohol-free wine and lager can be used for cooking if necessary.
- Reduce the consumption of alcohol – use non or low alcohol products, or low-calorie soft drinks.

The following foods commonly appear in questions where menus or foods have to be adapted. Here are some suggestions for adaptation to help you:

Ingredient/food	Adaptation	Comments
Bread/sandwich/toast	Use wholemeal varieties	Adds NSP to the diet
Butter/margarine	Polyunsaturated margarine/low fat spread	Reduces fat (including saturated fat) content of diet. Polyunsaturated fat is better for health than saturated fats.
Whole milk	Skimmed or semi-skimmed milk	Reduces fat (including saturated fat) content of the diet
Plain flour/Self-raising (SR) flour	Wholemeal flour/ wholemeal SR flour	Adds NSP to the diet
Cheddar cheese/cheese	Low fat cheese/edam	Reduces fat (including saturated fat) content of the diet
Sugary drink	Water/low fat milk/fresh fruit juice	Reduces the sugar intake of the diet. Milk will add important nutrients (see previous section). Fruit juice helps meet the target for increasing fruit intake.
Snacks (e.g. crisps)	Piece of fruit	Reduces fat and salt content whilst helping with fruit target
	Low fat crisps	Reduces the fat content of the diet
	Low salt crisps	Reduces the salt content of the diet
Biscuits/cakes	Piece of fruit	Reduces sugar content while helping to meet fruit target
	Plain biscuit/cake or wholemeal varieties	Can reduce the fat and sugar intake. Wholemeal versions also increase NSP content of the diet.

It is also important to remember that, as well as adapting the types of food you use when preparing meals, you can select cookery methods which will help meet current dietary advice.

Choice of cooking methods

There are a number of cooking methods which can be used to help meet current dietary advice. Remember that not all methods of cooking are suitable for all types of foods. There are some methods of cooking which should be used less frequently because they increase the fat content of the food.

Method of cooking	Fat is added	No fat is added	Fat is removed	Nutrients are lost
Grilling		•	•	some
Baking		•		some
Boiling		•		little
Shallow frying	•			some
Stir frying	little			
Deep frying	•			some
Steaming		•		
Microwave cooking		•		
Pressure cooking		•		
Poaching		•		

Some methods of cooking will add fat to foods during cooking, whilst others will help remove fat.

Some methods of cooking will remove nutrients from cooking – especially Vitamins B and C, which are water soluble and not stable when subjected to heat.

Alkalinity, solubility and heat affect the nutritive content of food

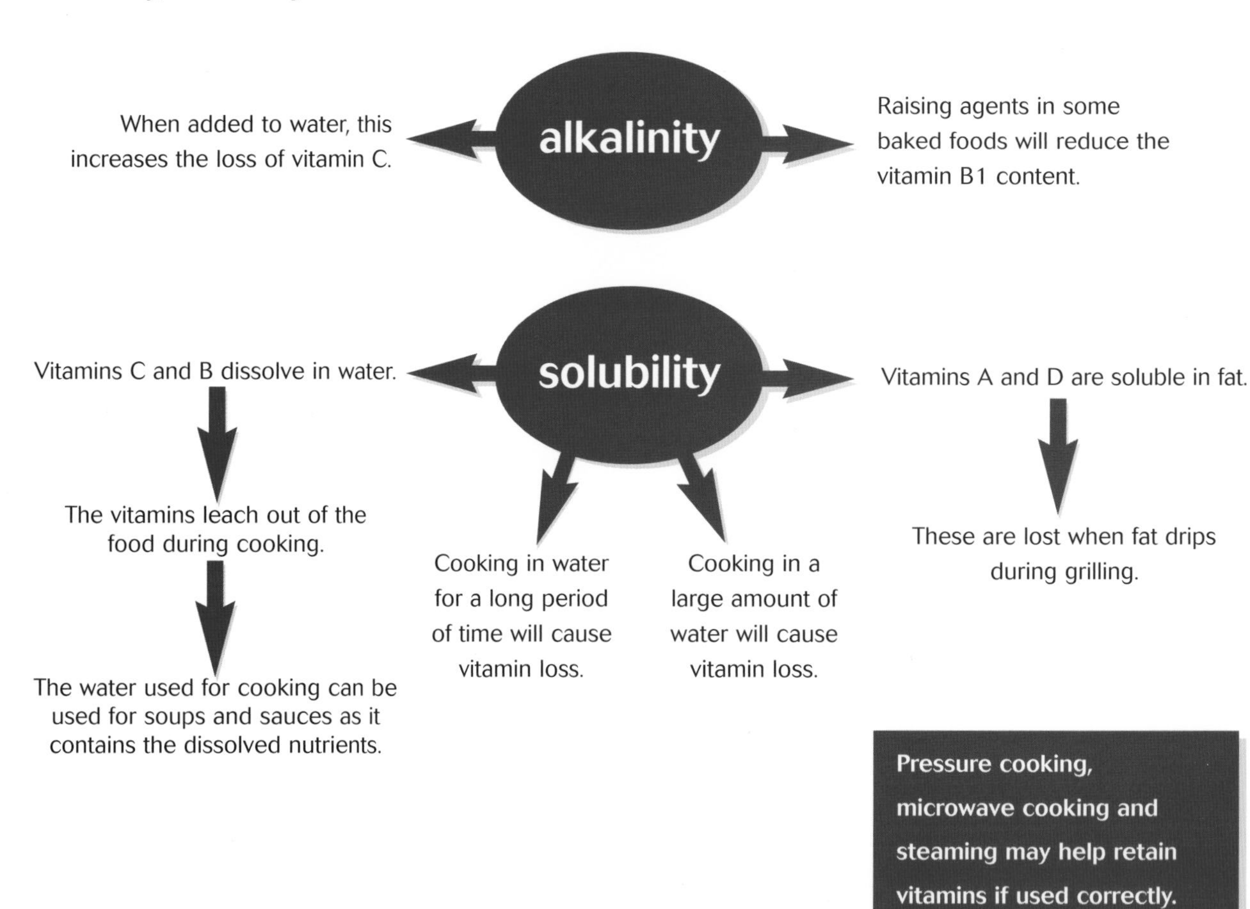

Pressure cooking, microwave cooking and steaming may help retain vitamins if used correctly.

Vitamin B is destroyed at high temperatures.

heat

Vitamin C is sensitive to low temperatures.

Relationship between diet and health

Eating a diet which meets the Scottish dietary targets will help to prevent a wide range of illnesses and so help to develop good health.

Anaemia

Anaemia is mainly caused by
- not having enough iron (iron deficiency)
- not having enough vitamin B12 (B12 deficiency)
- not having enough folic acid (folic acid deficiency).

Red blood cells contain a substance called haemoglobin. This carries oxygen in the blood.
'Anaemia' means that the level of red cells and haemoglobin in the blood is abnormally low. As a result, the oxygen-carrying capacity of the blood is reduced.

The symptoms of anaemia depend on the type of deficiency:

Iron deficient anaemia	Vitamin B12 deficient anaemia	Folic acid deficient anaemia
• tiredness • breathlessness • dizziness (especially when standing) and a weak, rapid pulse	• damage to nerves (abnormal sensation and movement) • sore tongue • pigmented skin • colour blindness • depression, confusion and decreased intellectual function	• foetal malformations (including spina bifida) • neurological abnormalities in infants
This is the most common form of anaemia.	This is normally called megaloblastic anaemia. Vitamin B12 is found only in animal products and so can be deficient in vegan diets.	Folic acid is required at the time of the development of a foetus and so is important for pregnant women.

Bowel disorders

There are many different types of bowel disorders that are linked to poor diet:
- constipation
- haemorrhoids (piles)
- cancer – of various parts of the digestive system
- diverticular disease – see section 'Relationship between water, non-starch polysaccharides and health' (page 15).

Constipation

This is the passage of hard and dry faeces (bowel movements) less than two/three times a week, associated with an uncomfortable abdominal feeling. The most common causes of constipation are a relative lack of NSP and liquids in the diet. The main treatment is a diet with enough NSP content (up to 35 grams a day).

Haemorrhoids (piles)

These are enlarged and engorged blood vessels in or around the back passage (anus), which may be associated with pain, bleeding, itching and feeling as if a lump or bump is hanging down. Piles are very common, especially in countries where the diet is highly processed and low in NSP.

It seems that the people most at risk of developing piles are those who have more cause for raised abdominal pressure, such as:
- those chronically straining with constipation
- after or during pregnancy
- overweight people
- people with heavy lifting jobs.

Piles are very common but can be prevented by:
- avoiding becoming overweight
- eating a diet high in NSP
- exercising regularly.

Cancer

The body is made up of many types of cells. Normally cells grow, divide, and produce more cells as they are needed to keep the body healthy and functioning properly. Sometimes, however, the process goes wrong and cells keep dividing when new cells are not needed. This leads to a tumour or cancer.

The colon and rectum are parts of the body's digestive system which remove nutrients from food and store waste until it passes out of the body. Colorectal cancer (cancers of the colon and/or rectum) seems to be associated with diets that are high in fat and calories and low in NSP.

There are a number of steps that should be taken which may prevent certain types of cancer:

- A diet rich in fruit, vegetables and whole grain cereals will provide the body with vitamins A, C and E, as well as providing NSP. All of these substances have roles in preventing the development of cancer.
- Eating large amounts of pickled, smoked or salted foods has been shown to have a link to the development of certain types of cancer and so should be consumed in moderation.
- Drinking alcohol appears to increase the chance of developing certain types of cancer. Consumption should be reduced to small amounts.

Coronary Heart Disease (CHD)

The heart needs a supply of blood if it is to function correctly. CHD occurs when fatty deposits, which stick to the artery walls, block the arteries that provide the heart with its supply of blood. This can lead to severe chest pain, a heart attack and possibly death. Cholesterol is one of the components of this fatty deposit.

RESTRICTED BLOOD FLOW IN ARTERY OF THE HEART

ARTERY WALL

FATTY DEPOSIT

Cholesterol is a soft, waxy substance found among the fats in the bloodstream and in all your body's cells. It's an important part of a healthy body because it's used to form cell membranes, some hormones and other needed tissues.

The level of cholesterol in the blood is linked with the development of these fatty deposits. If the level is high, the risks of CHD are generally high.

We can increase the amount of cholesterol in the diet by eating the wrong types of foods. Saturated fatty acids can raise blood cholesterol, which increases your risk of heart disease. Salt has also been shown to have a link with CHD (see hypertension section below).

There are a number of steps that should be taken which may prevent certain CHD:

- Reduce the intake of saturated fat in the diet.
- Antioxidants (vitamins A, C and E) in the diet may help to prevent CHD by stopping the fatty deposits from sticking to artery walls. Therefore their consumption should be increased.
- A change of diet from one which is high in saturated fat to one that is high in polyunsaturated fat may be beneficial. It is thought that polyunsaturated fatty acids may help reduce the tendency for blood to clot and so reduce the risk of heart attack.

There are other risk factors associated with CHD, as well as bad diet:

- cigarette smoking
- insufficient exercise
- family history
- high blood pressure
- stress
- obesity
- age
- gender
- alcohol.

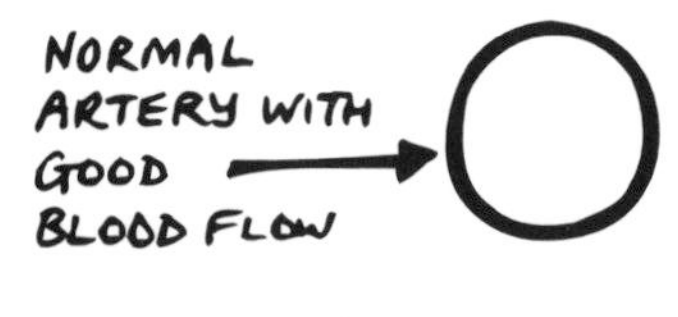

ARTERY WITH FATTY DEPOSITS LEADING TO INCREASED BLOOD PRESSURE AND POSSIBLE RISK OF BLOOD CLOT

Hypertension and strokes

Hypertension is another name for high blood pressure. High blood pressure directly increases the risk of CHD (which leads to heart attacks) and strokes, especially along with other risk factors. High blood pressure can lead to the thickening and hardening of artery walls. High blood pressure causes the heart to work harder than normal. This means both the heart and arteries are more prone to injury.

If high blood pressure isn't treated, the heart may have to work harder and harder to pump enough blood and oxygen around the body's organs and tissues to meet their needs. When the heart is forced to work harder than normal for an extended time, it tends to enlarge and weaken.

Arterial damage is bad because hardened or narrowed arteries may not be able to carry the amount of blood the body's organs need. If the body's organs don't get enough oxygen and nutrients, they can't work properly. Another risk is that a blood clot may lodge in an artery narrowed by fatty deposits, which then deprives part of the body of its normal blood supply. This can lead to a stroke, where the blood supply to the brain is interrupted or stopped.

There are a number of factors that contribute to high blood pressure, two of which are diet-related:

- Diet rich in sodium (salt)
  High sodium consumption increases the blood pressure of some people, leading to high blood pressure. People diagnosed with high blood pressure are often put on sodium-restricted diets.

- Obesity and overweight
  Studies have shown that body weight is related to changes in blood pressure levels. People who are overweight are more likely to have high blood pressure.

There are other risk factors associated with high blood pressure as well as bad diet:

- age
- gender
- family history
- race
- alcohol
- some medicines
- lack of exercise.

Tooth decay

Tooth decay is sometimes called dental caries.

When you eat, bits of food (some too small for you to see) remain in your mouth. They feed bacteria that grow in a sticky film on your teeth. This film, called plaque, is the main cause of tooth decay and gum disease. Bacteria produce acid which dissolves teeth, causing tooth decay. Brushing your teeth after meals and after between-meal snacks not only gets rid of the food particles that you can see but also removes plaque from your teeth. Using fluoride toothpaste is important because the fluoride can help kill bacteria, as well as make your teeth stronger. However diet is also important in preventing tooth decay.

If your diet is low in certain nutrients, it may be harder for the tissues of your mouth to resist infection. This may be a contributing factor to (gum) disease, the main cause of tooth loss in adults. A well-balanced diet will help maintain dental health. When you do snack, avoid soft, sweet, sticky foods, such as cakes, candy and dried fruits, that cling to your teeth and promote tooth decay. Instead, choose foods such as nuts, raw vegetables, plain yoghurt, cheese, unsalted and non-sweetened popcorn and sugarless gum or candy. Remember that fluoride has an important role to play in maintaining dental health.

Weight control and obesity

Being overweight is not itself a common cause of death; however it does increase the risk of a variety of medical conditions:

- CHD
- stroke
- certain cancers
- diabetes
- gall stones.

We all need energy for our bodies to function correctly. Even when sleeping, our bodies need energy to function. If you are very energetic, you will need more energy than if you are not. However, if you do not use all the energy that you consume in food, the extra is stored in the body as fat.

In the UK, being overweight is a common problem. Being excessively overweight is called obesity. The only ways to lose weight are to:

- eat fewer energy rich foods – particularly fatty foods
- take more exercise – which will burn extra energy.

To prevent obesity the following factors should be considered:

- Fat is a concentrated source of energy so eat fewer high fat foods (e.g. pies, cakes, confectionery).
- Intake of sugary foods should be reduced as they provide lots of energy, but few other nutrients.
- Starchy foods, fruits and vegetables, lean meat and low fat dairy products should form part of a low energy diet.
- Eating foods high in NSP will make you feel fuller for a longer period of time, and so your desire to eat will be reduced.

Food labelling

To the consumer, food labelling can be confusing, especially when trying to pick foods that can help contribute to following current dietary advice. Many use words like 'pure' and 'natural', but what does this really mean? There are laws and guidelines which mean that a standard format for nutrition labelling must be followed.

So what should you look for?

This allows you to compare the nutritive value of similar products

The amounts of each nutrient per 100g or per 100ml must be shown.

Manufacturers can display the energy, protein, carbohydrate and fat content of food.

Some may also show saturates, sugars, fibre, and sodium.

NUTRITION INFORMATION

TYPICAL VALUES	PER 90g DRAINED SERVING	PER 100g DRAINED PRODUCT
ENERGY	78kJ/18kcal	87kJ/20kcal
PROTEIN	0.6g	0.7g
CARBOHYDRATE	4.0g	4.4g
of which sugars	4.0g	4.4g
FAT	Nil	Nil
of which saturates	Nil	Nil
FIBRE	1.7g	1.9g
SODIUM	0.3g	0.3g

PER 90g DRAINED SERVING 18 CALORIES NIL FAT

This pack contains approximately 2 drained servings of 90g

Information can additionally be shown 'per serving' if the number of servings in the whole packet is given on the label.

At present, nutrition labelling is voluntary unless a manufacturer makes a claim about the product on the packet or in an advert.

The ingredients in a food product must be displayed on its food label. It is not always easy to understand the ingredients on a food label. The following ingredients may appear on a label: sucrose, lactose, glucose syrup. These are all forms of sugar. If you do not know what these ingredients are, you might not realise this product contains sugar.

Some companies have developed their own labelling systems, which assist consumers to make 'healthy choices'. For more information visit the following web sites:

http://www.co-op.co.uk
http://www.tesco.com/healthyeating

Individuals have varying dietary needs

Dietary requirements of different groups of individuals

Dietary requirements of groups with special needs

Factors affecting food choice →

Dietary requirements of different groups of individuals

No two people are alike. We all have different dietary requirements. There are, however, certain groups in society who have specific dietary needs.

The needs of individuals and groups in society are measured by Dietary Reference Values (DRVs). These are outlined in the charts below for different population groups. DRVs are subdivided into:

- Reference Nutrient Intake (RNI) – the amount of a nutrient that is sufficient for most of the population
- Estimated Average Requirement (EAR) – estimate of the average need for a nutrient. Some may need more, some may need less.
- Lower Reference Nutrient Intake (LRNI) – for those people who have low needs.

Infants

An infant's diet for the first few weeks of life is milk (whether breast or bottle-fed). Human milk is ideal for a number of reasons:

- It contains the correct composition and proportion of nutrients to ensure growth and development.
- It is of the correct temperature and consistency.
- The milk is easy to digest.
- It is free and convenient.
- It contains antibodies that can help fight infection.
- No preparation is required and so risk of contamination from bacteria is reduced.
- Breast feeding helps develop a bond between mother and child.

Age Range	Estimated Average Requirements	Reference Nutrient Intake									
	ENERGY kcal/day	PROTEIN g/day	VITAMIN A retinol equiv µg/day	THIAMIN mg/day	RIBOFLAVIN mg/day	NIACIN Nicotinic acid equiv mg/day	VITAMIN C mg/day	VITAMIN D µg/day	CALCIUM mg/day	IRON mg/day	SODIUM mg/day
Boys < 1	545–920	12·5–14·9	350	0·2–0·3	0·4	3–5	25	8·5 (0–6 mths)	525	1·7–7·8	210–350
Girls < 1	515–865	12·5–14·9	350	0·2–0·3	0·4	3–5	25	8·5 (0–6 mths)	525	1·7–7·8	210–350

Children

As childhood is a time of fast growth and development there is an increased demand for all nutrients.

Nutrient	Dietary Need
Protein	Protein is required for the growth, maintenance and repair of body tissues.
Total complex carbohydrate	This is a period of activity and children will require energy. To meet current dietary targets, starchy carbohydrates should be the main source of energy. All children require a source of fat. Children under five should not be given skimmed milk as it has a lower fat content and less of the fat soluble vitamins (A and D).
Calcium, vitamin D and phosphorus	As this is a period of growth and development, calcium, vitamin D and phosphorus are required to ensure correct bone development.
Iron	Iron is essential for healthy blood. Increased activity means the body cells require more oxygen. This is carried by the red blood cells, which need iron to carry the oxygen.
Vitamin C	Essential for absorption of iron as well as for maintaining the body's connective tissue.
Fluoride	To ensure protection for developing teeth.

Age Range	Estimated Average Requirements	Reference Nutrient Intake (RNI)									
	ENERGY kcal/day	PROTEIN g/day	VITAMIN A retinol equiv µg/day	THIAMIN mg/day	RIBOFLAVIN mg/day	NIACIN Nicotinic acid equiv mg/day	VITAMIN C mg/day	VITAMIN D µg/day	CALCIUM mg/day	IRON mg/day	SODIUM mg/day
Boys 1–3	1230	14·5	400	0·5	0·6	8	30	7·0 (6mths-3yrs)	350	6·9	500
Boys 4–6	1715	19·7	500	0·7	0·8	11	30	–	450	6·1	700
Boys 7–10	1970	28·3	500	0·7	1	12	30	–	550	8·7	1200
Girls 1–3	1165	14·5	400	0·5	0·6	8	30	7·0 (6mths-3yrs)	350	6·9	500
Girls 4–6	1545	19·7	500	0·7	0·8	11	30	–	450	6·1	700
Girls 7–10	1740	28·3	500	0·7	1	12	30	–	550	8·7	1200

Adolescents

This is a period of rapid growth and body development. For this reason, nutritional requirements will increase. In particular, the following nutrients will be important:

Nutrient	Dietary Need
Protein	This is a period of sometimes rapid growth and so protein is required for the growth, maintenance and repair of body tissues.
Carbohydrate	Due to the larger body frame at this time of development, energy requirements will increase. Energy needs will vary from individual to individual depending on how active they are.
Iron	This is important for teenage girls in particular who, due to the onset of menstruation, will require increased sources of iron to prevent anaemia.

Age Range	Estimated Average Requirements	Reference Nutrient Intake									
	ENERGY kcal/day	PROTEIN g/day	VITAMIN A retinol equiv µg/day	THIAMIN mg/day	RIBOFLAVIN mg/day	NIACIN Nicotinic acid equiv mg/day	VITAMIN C mg/day	VITAMIN D µg/day	CALCIUM mg/day	IRON mg/day	SODIUM mg/day
Boys 11–14	2200	42·1	600	0·9	1·2	15	35	–	1000	11·3	1600
Boys 15–18	2755	55·2	700	1·1	1·3	18	40	–	1000	11·3	1600
Girls 11–14	1845	41·2	600	0·7	1·1	12	35	–	800	14·8	1600
Girls 15–18	2110	45·4	600	0·8	1·1	14	40	–	800	14·8	1600

Adults

At this stage, body growth has declined so nutrients are required for maintenance and repair purposes. Individual nutrient requirements will depend on a variety of individual factors, discussed in the next section.

Age Range	Estimated Average Requirements	Reference Nutrient Intake									
	ENERGY kcal/day	PROTEIN g/day	VITAMIN A retinol equiv µg/day	THIAMIN mg/day	RIBOFLAVIN mg/day	NIACIN Nicotinic acid equiv mg/day	VITAMIN C mg/day	VITAMIN D µg/day	CALCIUM mg/day	IRON mg/day	SODIUM mg/day
Men 19–50	2550	55·5	700	1·0	1·3	17	40	–	700	8·7	1600
Men 50+	2550	53·3	700	0·9	1·3	16	40	(65+ µg/day)	700	8·7	1600
Women 19–50	1940	45	600	0·8	1·1	13	40	–	700	14·8	1600
Women 50+	1900	46·5	600	0·8	1·1	12	40	(65+ µg/day)	700	8·7	1600

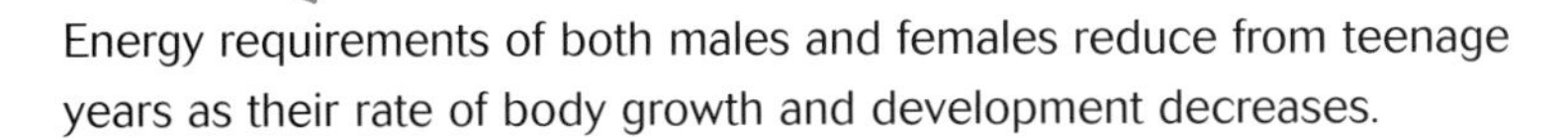

Energy requirements of both males and females reduce from teenage years as their rate of body growth and development decreases.

The requirement for iron decreases as the menstrual loss of blood stops.

Elderly People

The number of elderly people in the UK is increasing. Elderly people generally become less active, requiring less energy than their younger counterparts. It is important to ensure that meals are still well-planned and balanced to ensure that the correct nutrients are available in the correct proportions for the maintenance and repair of the body. There are a number of diet-related problems that can occur in later life.

Diet Related Problem	Dietary Advice
Constipation	The diet should have an adequate amount of NSP. It is also important that sufficient liquid is consumed.
Anaemia	The diet should have sufficient sources of iron and vitamin C.
Bone disorders	A diet rich in calcium, vitamin D and phosphorus is advised to prevent bone disorders.
Digestive problems	• Some elderly people have false teeth, which can make chewing some foods difficult. With careful planning of meals such problems can be overcome. • Digesting fatty foods can be a problem. Foods and cooking methods should be selected carefully.

Osteoporosis is a disease in which bones become fragile and more likely to break. Women are four times more likely than men to develop this disease. There is no cure, but it can be prevented by a balanced diet rich in calcium and vitamin D; exercise using weights and by following a healthy lifestyle with no smoking or excessive alcohol use.

Osteomalacia means 'soft bones'. This softening is caused by loss of calcium from the skeleton. This has a number of causes, one of which is poor diet.

Credit Only

Dietary requirements of groups with special needs

The following groups have particular dietary requirements.

Pregnant women

It is important that women who are planning to become pregnant or are already pregnant follow a healthy balanced diet.

Nutrient	Dietary Need
Protein	Additional protein will be required for the development of the foetus's body cells.
Carbohydrate	In the last three months of pregnancy, the body has a greater requirement for energy. This is a time of rapid growth and movement for the developing foetus. It is important, however, not to take in too much energy, otherwise additional weight gain may occur and this can lead to complications.
Iron	The loss of blood via menstruation ceases during pregnancy so an increased intake of iron is not considered necessary. It is important, however, that iron intake is maintained as this will supply the newly born baby with sufficient iron to last it through the first few weeks of life.
Vitamin C	Foods rich in vitamin C should be in the diet to enable iron to be absorbed. Extra vitamin C is needed to help the baby's tissue formation.
Folic Acid	It is important that sufficient foods containing folic acid are consumed before and during pregnancy – especially in the first three months. Folic acid reduces the risk of babies being born with neural tube defects such as spina bifida. Folic acid supplements may be advised by a doctor or midwife.
Calcium, vitamin D and phosphorus	A baby's bones contain about 30g of calcium at the time of birth. This calcium is provided by the mother's diet. It is important that calcium intake is maintained to ensure that calcium deposits from the mother's bones are not used for this purpose.

Many women find that constipation and piles occur during pregnancy. A diet rich in NSP will help prevent such problems. It is also important to keep drinking water, which can also help prevent constipation.

hazard

Eating liver and liver pâté should be avoided during pregnancy. These food items contain rich amounts of vitamin A. Whilst the body requires vitamin A for healthy skin and vision, too much can be harmful to the developing baby.

Other food that should also be avoided during pregnancy include: soft cheeses such as Brie and Camembert; pâté; and cook-chill foods. These products may contain listeria bacteria, which can harm the developing baby.

Other foods such as raw eggs (and foods containing raw eggs) may contain salmonella bacteria, which can harm a developing baby.

Vegetarians

There are many different types of vegetarians. In your Standard Grade Home Economics examination, there are two main types that you have to know about:

- Lactovegetarians
  Lactovegetarians do not eat meat or meat products, including eggs and fish, but do eat milk, cheese and other dairy products.

- Vegans
  Vegans do not eat any animal-derived products, including eggs, milk, cheese and other dairy products.

There are different reasons why people become vegetarians:

Reason	Explanation
Religion	Some religions have rules about the types of foods that can be eaten. For some religions these rules can be very strict. Many Hindus and Buddhists are vegetarians, although eating some forms of meat is not actually forbidden.
Moral issues	Some people believe that it is wrong to kill animals for food. Others believe that it is not environmentally friendly to use animals for food, as it is an expensive way to produce food.
Health	Some people may follow a vegetarian diet for health-related reasons.
Taste	Some people do not like the taste or texture of meat.
Peer pressure	Some people – particularly younger people – may become vegetarian as a result of pressure from friends.

For whatever reason a person becomes a vegetarian, there are a number of factors that they need to consider when planning meals to ensure that they do not become deficient in certain nutrients.

Should have few problems achieving a balanced diet, as three protein foods are still available in the diet.

Can obtain most nutrients from plant sources except for vitamin B12. Foods which are fortified (have nutrients added to them) with vitamin B12 should be consumed.

Protein is found in varying amounts in plant sources. As these will be LBV proteins, a combination must be taken to make up the shortage of essential amino acids in each.

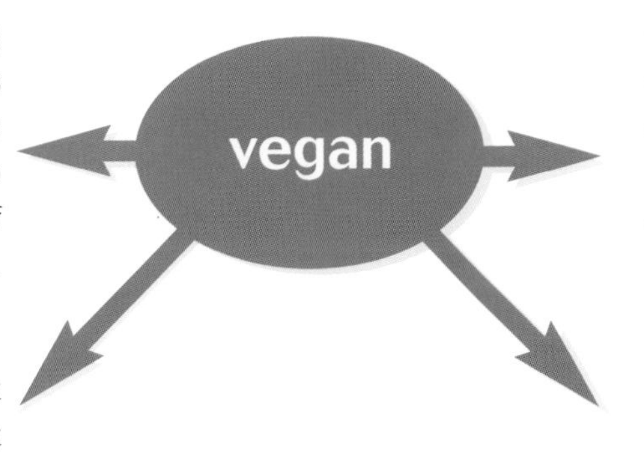

Calcium may be deficient – this can be provided by pulses, nuts and fruits and vegetables. The presence of phytic acid may make some calcium unavailable to the body.

Vitamin D is found in few plant foods. Sunlight is an important source.

For vegans, the higher intake of NSP will have a positive effect on health, as more pulses, nuts, fruits and vegetables are consumed. The saturated fat content of the diet should also reduce as more polyunsaturated fats are consumed. A vegan diet may also increase the TCC intake of the diet.

Soya can be used to make textured vegetable protein and Tofu. This is a plant source of protein, but has a HBV protein content. It is ideal for inclusion in a vegetarian diet.

Available in pieces, minced and in many foods such as burgers, sausages and ready meals, making it very useful for the diet of a vegetarian.

Mycoprotein (e.g. Quorn) is made from a plant source and is ideal for most vegetarian diets.* It is high in protein, low in fat and is a source of NSP.

* Mycoprotein often uses egg albumen as a binder and so may not be suitable for some vegetarians.

Factors affecting food choice

There are a number of common factors that affect the dietary requirements and choice of food for individuals, other than those specifically described above.

Body size

Not everyone has the same body size. We all know people who can eat lots of food but still remain slim. We all know people who just need to look at a cream cake, and the pounds seem to pile on! The amount of energy a person needs is determined by their basal metabolic rate (BMR). This is the amount of energy needed when the body is resting, and energy is only required to keep the body functioning – to keep the heart pumping and the lungs breathing. Tall, thin people have higher BMRs. People with a lot of fatty tissue tend to have a lower BMR. Those with a higher BMR will burn energy quickly.

Age

Our nutritional requirements vary as we grow and develop. In youth, the BMR is higher because age brings less lean body mass and slows the BMR. As well as energy differences, the amounts of other nutrients will differ throughout life, as discussed in the previous section. As we age, we generally become less active so requirements for energy reduce.

Gender (male or female)

Men tend to have larger body sizes and so require more protein for the development of additional muscle tissue. Because of this larger body size, energy requirements are greater.

Available income

The amount of income available for purchasing food and food preparation equipment will have a significant effect on the types of food purchased, and so on the nutrients gained from this food. The amount of income available to spend on food not only affects the quantity of food purchased but also the type of food purchased. As people earn more money, it is generally found that the intake of animal protein and saturated fat intake increases. It is also known that where income is limited, people eat less fresh fruit and vegetables.

Health

There are a number of health factors that affect dietary requirements and food choice. We have already looked at pregnancy and vegetarianism. However, there are other health factors that should be considered.

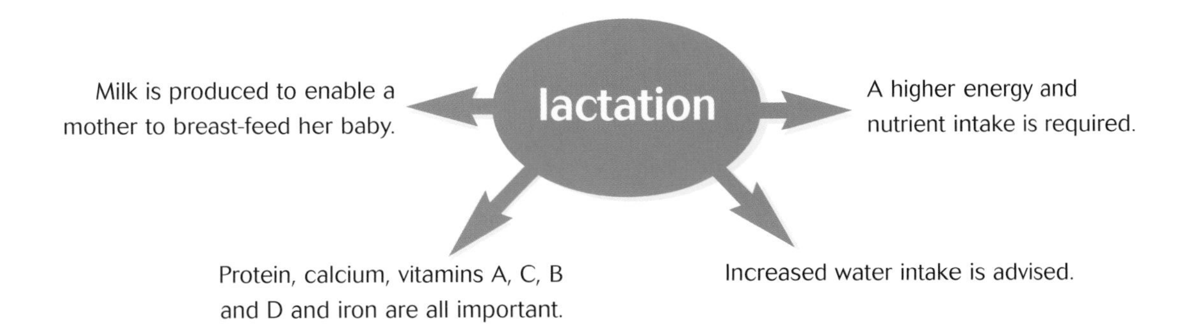

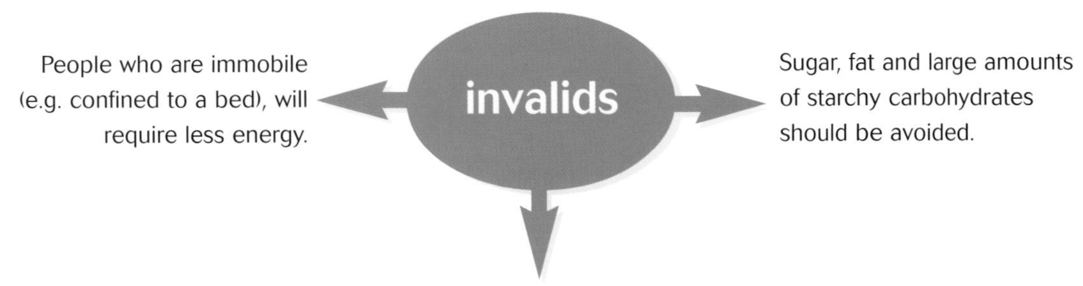

The requirement for nutrients to maintain and repair body tissues becomes important – protein, calcium, iron and vitamins A, D and C for example.

Lifestyle/activities/occupation

The amount of energy people use in physical activity varies according to their occupation, lifestyle and the activities they are involved in.

Active People

- More energy is needed to allow muscles to receive the required amounts of energy to function well.
- More protein is needed for growth, maintenance and repair of body tissues.
- B vitamins are needed to release energy from carbohydrates and fats.
- Iron and vitamin C are needed to allow oxygen to be transported to the body tissues.
- An increased number of antioxidant vitamins are needed to protect cells and tissues during exercise.
- Extra fluids are needed to replace those lost during perspiration.
- Additional sodium is needed to replace that lost through perspiration.

Less Active People

- Will require fewer energy-rich foods during the working day, as their jobs are not physically demanding.
- Will have no increased requirements for other nutrients during the working day.
- Although the person may have a non-physical job, he or she may be involved in active hobbies. This will affect their nutritional requirement.

In your Standard Grade Home Economics exam, you may be asked to evaluate the diet of a specific person. Remember to:

- Think about the activities that the person will be involved in.
- Think about each of the major nutrients as well as NSP.
- Think about the function of each nutrient.
- Decide whether this person will need an additional requirement or not.

- Think what might happen to the person if they did not get enough of each nutrient.
- Think about what might happen to the person if they got too much of each nutrient.

The key to success in these types of questions is to know the sources and functions of all the nutrients.

Cleanliness is important in relation to health

General personal hygiene
Clothes care
Hygiene in relation to food handling
Causes, effects and control of food spoilage
Food storage and preservation
Food poisoning
Cross-contamination of food
Refrigerators and freezers →

General personal hygiene

Good personal hygiene is important as it will help to boost your self-confidence and make you feel good. It will also help to create a good impression with other people. Good personal hygiene is all about taking care of your body.

Bacteria are organisms that live all around us. They are so small that they cannot be seen by the naked eye. Bacteria live and grow on our bodies, but we cannot see them. Your skin has tiny pores, which help to get rid of waste products from the body. Bacteria can thrive on these waste products. The end result of this is that your skin may begin to smell. This is called body odour.

Simple steps for good personal hygiene:

- Wash daily – this removes stale sweat and bacteria that can cause odours.
- Brush teeth twice a day – this prevents tooth decay and keeps your breath from smelling.
- Visit the dentist for regular check-ups and change your toothbrush on a regular basis.
- Wash hands after visiting the toilet and before each meal. This prevents the spread of bacteria.
- Brush or comb your hair daily – this helps remove dead skin cells and stimulates the flow of blood to the hair roots.
- Wash your hair on a regular basis – particularly if it is greasy.
- Take care of your eyes – visit the optician if you are having eye problems.
- You use your feet daily. Take care of them and visit a chiropodist or doctor if you are experiencing foot problems.

Clothes care

Just as it is important to take care of your skin, it is important to take care of your clothes. Like the skin, clothing can contain many bacteria. Bacteria can thrive on clothing that has absorbed perspiration and spills. Clothing can also soak up odours, such as cooking odours and cigarette smoke. You may look good, but if your clothing does not look or smell good, all your efforts are wasted.

Clothing should be:

- washed on a regular basis
- dried properly
- ironed when necessary
- stored correctly.

It is important to know how to care for your clothing correctly. For this reason, a care labelling system is used to give instructions to ensure that clothing is laundered correctly. All garments have a care label attached to them, similar to the one shown opposite. Washing machine instruction booklets also display these symbols.

This system gives instructions on how to wash, bleach, iron, dry clean and dry clothing. This system is used internationally, so any clothing that is imported into this country, or any clothing bought abroad, will use this same system to provide laundering instructions.

Washing symbols

The wash tub symbol is used to give instructions on how to wash clothing.

There is a series of wash tub symbols for clothing made from different fibres. This symbol gives two types of information:

The wash temperature is indicated below the water line

The amount of washing machine agitation required for the garment is indicated by a bar below the wash tub symbol

Maximum wash temperature	Wash instructions	Suitable fabrics
Very Hot 95°C	Maximum machine action. Rinse and spin.	White cotton and linen articles without special finishes.
Hot 60°C	Maximum machine action. Rinse and spin.	Cotton, linen or viscose articles, without special finishes where colours are fast at 60°C.
Hand hot 50°C	Medium machine action. Rinse with gradual cooling, reduced spin or drip dry.	Nylon, polyester cotton mixes, polyester cotton and viscose with special finishes, cotton and acrylic mixes.
Warm 40°C	Maximum machine action. Rinse and spin.	Cotton, linen or viscose articles where colours are fast at 40°C but not at 60°C.
Warm 40°C	Medium machine action. Rinse with gradual cooling, reduced spin or drip dry.	Acrylics, acetates and triacetate, including mixtures with wool, polyester and wool blends.
Warm 40°C	Minimum action, normal rinse and spin.	Wool, wool mixed with other fibres, silk.
Hand wash only	Look at the garment label for further instructions.	
Do not wash		

No bar mear
normal machi
action require

Solid bar mea
reduced
machine actic
required

Broken bar
means muc
reduced
machine acti
required

NOTE Some fabrics have special finishes (e.g. flame proof finishes). It is important to read carefully the care label on the garment for such items.

NOTE The dyes used in some fabrics may start to run at certain temperatures. Where a label states colourfast at 60°C this means that the garment can be washed at this temperature without the dye running. You should read the care label instructions carefully for strongly coloured items.

Bleaching symbols

Bleach is used to remove stains and soiling from clothing and fabrics. Bleach is usually only used on white fabric.

Bleaching instructions are recognised by this triangle symbol.

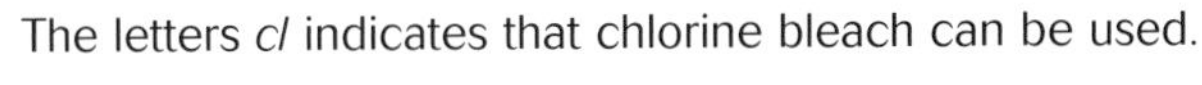

This symbol indicates that the clothing or fabric can be bleached.
The letters *cl* indicates that chlorine bleach can be used.

A symbol with a cross through it means 'do not'. In this case the symbol means do not bleach.

Drying symbols

It is relatively easy to dry clothes. However, some items of clothing contain fibres that need to be dried in a particular way to make sure the fibres (and so the clothing) are not damaged.

Drying instructions are recognised by a square symbol.

This symbol means that clothing can be tumble-dried.

This symbol means that clothing should not be tumble-dried.

This symbol means that the clothing should be dried flat, i.e. you should not hang this clothing on a washing line.

This symbol means that clothing can be line-dried, i.e. you can hang this item on a washing line.

This symbol means that the clothing should be drip dried, i.e. it is better to hang the clothing when it is still wet.

Ironing symbols

Many items of clothing crease during washing and drying. Passing some dry or moist heat over the fibres of the clothing smoothes out any creases. It is important however to know how hot the iron should be – too hot and the clothing may burn or melt, too cool and the clothing will remain creased.

This symbol indicates how the clothing should be ironed. There are four iron symbols.

A HOT iron is required (210°C). Used for clothing made from cotton and linen.

A WARM iron is required (160°C). Used for clothing made from wool, silk, polyester mixes.

A COOL iron is required (120°C). Used for clothing made from nylon, polyester, acrylics, acetate, tricel and viscose.

This symbol means that the clothing should not be ironed.

Dry cleaning symbols

Some clothing cannot be cleaned in the normal way – using water and detergent. Some grease and stubborn stains are difficult to remove with water and detergent. In these cases, dry cleaning is used.

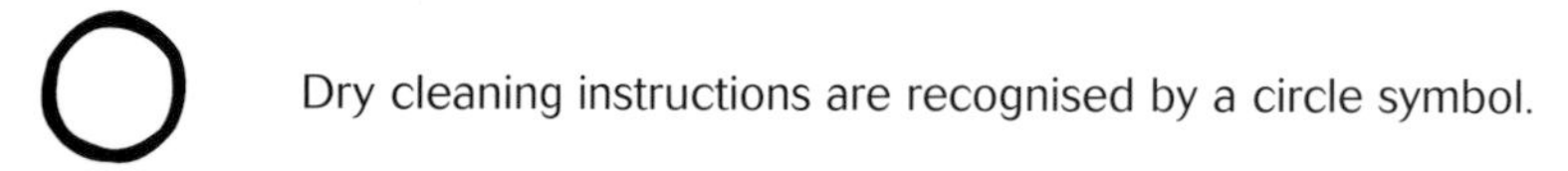

Dry cleaning instructions are recognised by a circle symbol.

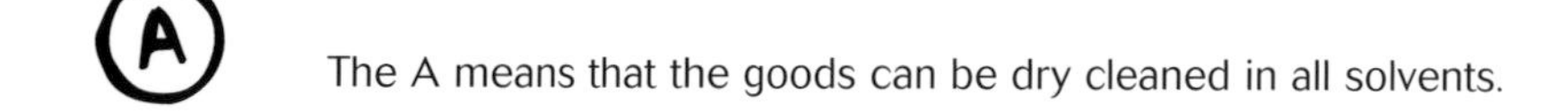

The A means that the goods can be dry cleaned in all solvents.

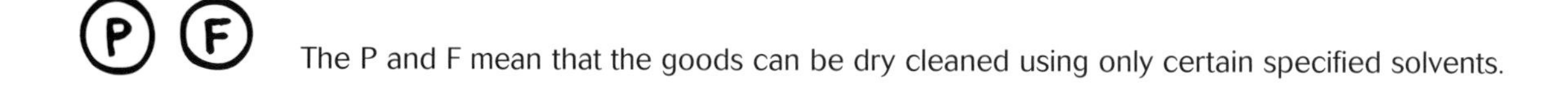

The P and F mean that the goods can be dry cleaned using only certain specified solvents.

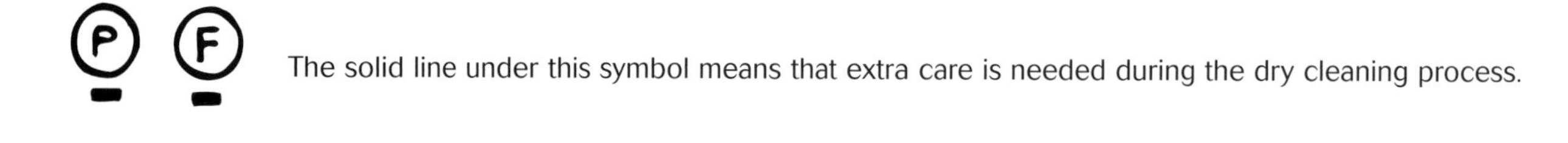

The solid line under this symbol means that extra care is needed during the dry cleaning process.

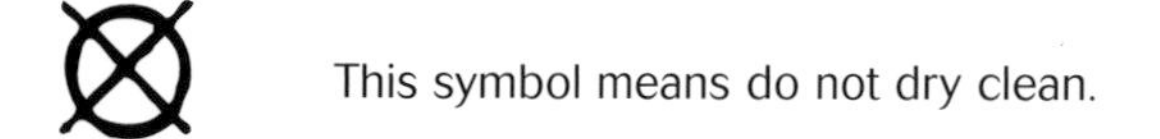

This symbol means do not dry clean.

Please note that the symbols A, F and P are for use by professional dry cleaners only. It is not necessary to know the specific dry cleaning solvents used.

Hygiene in relation to food handling

Food hygiene is all about making sure that food is safe to eat. There are a number of rules that should be followed when preparing and cooking food to make sure it is safe to eat. These rules are listed below. The list is not exhaustive, but in your examination it would be unlikely that you would be asked to provide more than six different hygiene measures.

Hygiene can be split into two main categories:

hygiene

Hygiene linked to the person handling the food → **Personal Hygiene**

Hygiene linked to the environment → **Kitchen Hygiene**

Personal Hygiene	Kitchen Hygiene
Jewellery must not be worn. • Jewellery can be a breeding ground for bacteria. • Stones can fall out of jewellery and contaminate the food.	All waste must be disposed of correctly. • This prevents spread of bacteria and the infestation of pests. • Waste bins should have well-fitting lids.
Cuts, spots, boils and skin infections are breeding grounds for bacteria. • They should be covered with waterproof plasters. • The plasters should be coloured so they are visible if they fall off.	Separate washing facilities for hands and food. • This prevents the spread of bacteria. • Ideally disposable cloths used for cleaning. • Separate cloths for hand drying and equipment drying.
Hands and nails must remain clean. • Hands are in continual contact with food and can spread bacteria. • Nail varnish must be removed – it may flake into the food. • Hands should be washed on a regular basis, especially after visiting the toilet.	Food preparation areas must be clean and well maintained. • Toilet facilities should be located well away from the food preparation area. • Surfaces should be easy to clean. • Lighting should allow for good visibility to make cleaning effective.
Hair must be tied back and covered completely. This prevents hair strands falling into food.	Food should be covered at all times to prevent contamination with bacteria.
Clean protective clothing must be worn • to cover normal clothing and so prevent spread of bacteria. • only in the food preparation and cooking area and washed on a daily basis.	A 'clean-as-you-go' approach should always be adopted. • Spills should be wiped up immediately – these not only attract bacteria, but can be a safety hazard. • All work surfaces should be cleaned before and after use. • All equipment should be cleaned after use.
Health issues must be considered. • Coughing and sneezing associated with colds can spread bacteria to food. • Disposable paper tissues should be used and hands should be washed on a regular basis. • All health problems should be reported to a supervisor.	Animals must not be allowed in food preparation areas. • Animals are carriers of many bacteria and must be excluded from food preparation areas. • Any infestation of pests (e.g. flies) should be reported to a supervisor/Environmental Health Officer.

If you get a question in your exam to do with hygiene, read the question carefully to see if it specifies personal or kitchen hygiene. If it does not mention either, your answers can be from either personal or kitchen hygiene.

Causes, effects and control of food spoilage

Food spoilage is the process that leads to food becoming changed in such a way as to make it unfit for human consumption. Food spoilage is caused by the action of enzymes and micro-organisms.

Enzymes

Enzymes are chemicals that are found in food. These chemicals have important uses in food. They can cause food to deteriorate in three main ways:

- ripening – They cause fruits and vegetables to ripen. Ripening continues until the food becomes inedible (e.g. bananas become dark brown and very soft in texture).
- browning – Enzymes can react with air causing the skin of certain foods, such as potatoes and apples, to discolour.
- oxidation – Enzymes can cause the loss of certain nutrients, such as vitamins A, C and B1, from food.

Micro-organisms

There are three main micro-organisms that you need to know about:

- bacteria
- moulds
- yeast.

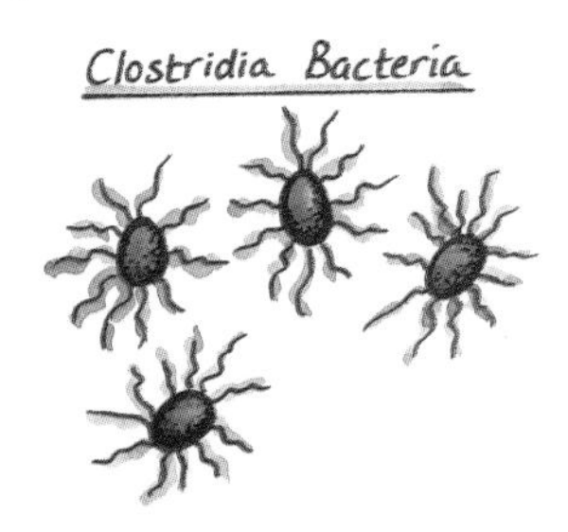

Bacteria are single-celled organisms that are so small they cannot be seen by the naked eye. Not all bacteria are bad for us. We have bacteria in our intestines but these bacteria are useful to us. Bacteria are also used in the manufacture of yoghurt and cheese. However, some bacteria can be harmful and it is these bacteria that can cause food to spoil and become dangerous to our health. Bacteria can be dangerous in three main ways:

- The presence of some bacteria in our food can lead to digestive upset.
- Some bacteria produce toxins (poisons) which can lead to digestive upset.
- Some bacteria can produce spores, which in turn can produce poisons.

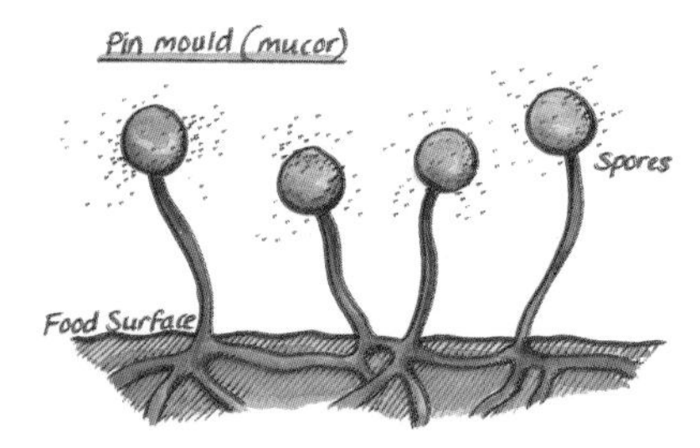

Moulds are a type of fungus that can cause food spoilage. Moulds produce spores, which can travel through the air. When they land on suitable food they begin to grow and multiply. Mould can be visible to the naked eye, such as moulds on bread. Certain types of moulds can produce poisons which will upset the digestive system. Not all moulds cause food spoilage. Moulds are used in some cheeses, such as Stilton, giving a characteristic colour and flavour.

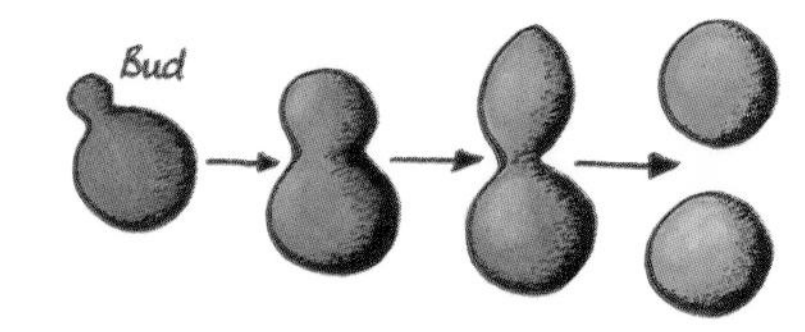

Yeast is also a type of fungus, which is found in the air and soil as well as on the surface of some fruits. Yeast can cause food spoilage in certain types of foods, such as jams and meats. They cause food spoilage as they can affect the taste of food. Not all types of yeast are harmful. Yeast is used in the production of bread and wine.

Conditions for bacterial growth

All micro-organisms require certain conditions to survive and reproduce. These conditions are:

When all of these conditions are present, they produce a chain of events that can lead to the growth and multiplication of bacteria. This in turn causes food spoilage and possible food poisoning.

Temperature

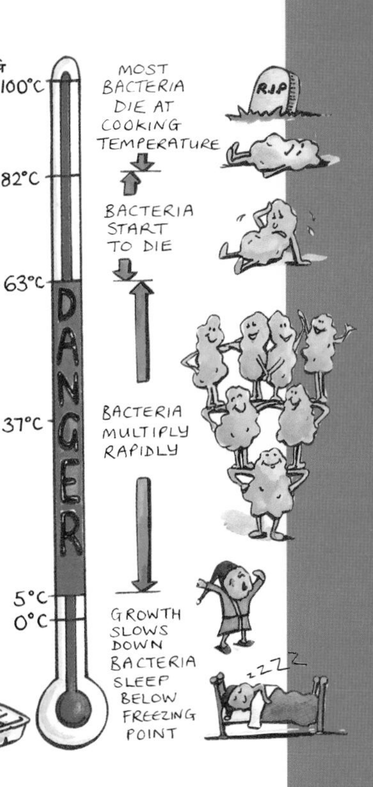

Bacteria need warm conditions to grow and multiply. The ideal temperature zone for bacterial growth is between 30°C and 37°C. Some bacteria can still grow at temperatures between 10°C and 60°C. For this reason we often say that the danger zone for bacterial growth is between 5°C and 63°C.

Most bacteria are destroyed at temperatures above 63°C. However, some bacteria produce spores when conditions for growth become poor. Spores can survive for long periods of time until conditions for growth become ideal, when they can begin to germinate and produce new bacteria.

At temperatures below 5°C (the usual temperature of a domestic fridge) bacteria find it difficult to grow and multiply. At very cold temperatures, bacteria become dormant – they do not die, but they cannot grow or multiply.

Food

Bacteria require a source of food if they are to grow and multiply. These foods usually contain large amounts of water and nutrients. Examples of suitable foods include:

- meat and meat products
- milk and dairy products
- fruit.

Moisture

Bacteria require moisture if they are to grow and multiply. Bacteria cannot grow where there is no moisture. It is important to remember that both moulds and bacteria can produce spores, which can survive in dried foods, until such a time when they are rehydrated.

Time

Bacteria require time if they are to grow and multiply. One bacterium can split into two every 20 minutes. In seven hours, the number of bacteria would reach several million. Foods which spoil very quickly are called perishable foods.

Oxygen

Some bacteria require oxygen if they are to grow and multiply. These bacteria are known as aerobic bacteria. Other bacteria grow best if there is no oxygen present. These are known as anaerobic bacteria.

pH

The pH of a substance is a measurement of how acidic or alkaline it is. A pH of 1 means the substance is very acidic. A pH of 14 means the substance is very alkaline. Most bacteria prefer pH conditions of between pH 6·6 and pH 7·5, i.e. neither very alkaline nor very acidic.

Moulds and yeast can survive at pH levels of 1–1·5. Food spoilage in these foods, such as fruits, is usually caused by yeast and moulds.

The important rule of food safety

If any one of the links in the food spoilage chain is broken, there is less chance of food spoilage happening.

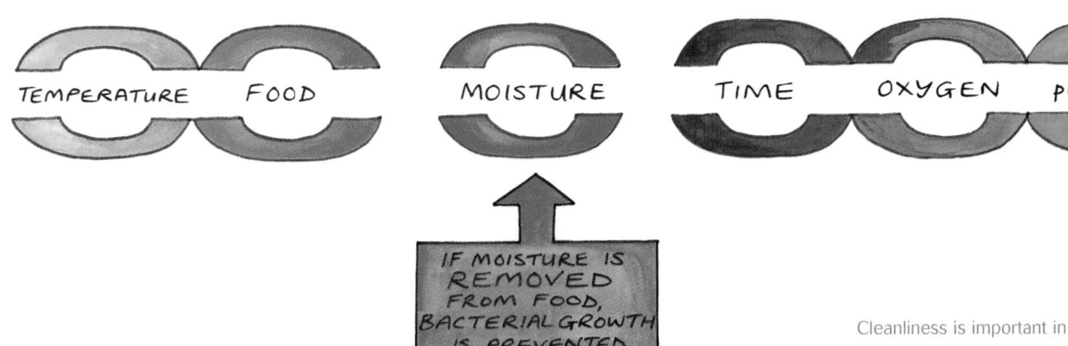

Food storage and preservation

The preservation of food is a process whereby control of temperature, food, moisture, time, oxygen and/or pH level are used to prevent food from spoiling.

Method of preservation	Description and comments	Suitable foods
Freezing	• Domestic freezing involves the use of temperatures of −22°C to −18°C. This very cold temperature makes bacteria dormant and so food spoilage is reduced. • Water changes to ice and so the amount of available moisture required for growth is reduced. • Some fruits and vegetables are blanched (dipped into very hot water for a very short time) before freezing. This destroys the enzymes that can make food spoil. NOTE: once food is defrosted, bacterial growth will increase.	Meat, chicken, fish, vegetables. Most foods can be frozen for periods of up to 18 months. Foods with a very high water content are not suitable for freezing. Dairy products tend not to freeze well.
Chilling	• Food is stored at a temperature above freezing – usually between 0°C and 4°C. This low temperature slows down the rate of bacterial multiplication and spoilage is also slowed down but not stopped. • Moulds can still grow in cold temperatures.	Chilled ready-to-eat foods, salad items, dairy produce, meat, fish.
Jam/marmalade making	• The initial boiling of the fruit will destroy enzymes, preventing later spoilage. • The initial boiling of the fruit will destroy micro-organisms (but not spores) preventing later spoilage. • The high concentration of sugar added during the jam making process reduces bacterial growth due to its dehydrating effect. • The jam bottles are normally heated before jam is added. This process destroys micro-organisms found in the jars.	Most berry fruits, black and red currants, plums, apricots, oranges, grapefruit.
Pickling/ chutney making	• The initial boiling of the ingredients will destroy enzymes, preventing later spoilage. • The initial boiling of the ingredients will destroy micro-organisms (but not spores) preventing later spoilage. • The high concentration of acid (vinegar) prevents bacterial growth and multiplication. • The pickle/chutney bottles are normally heated before the product is added. This process destroys micro-organisms found in the bottles.	Many fruits and vegetables can be used to make pickles and chutney. Some fish (e.g. herring) can be pickled.
Vacuum packaging	• Normally used in conjunction with chilling. • Oxygen is removed and so micro-organisms cannot multiply unless they are anaerobic. Sometimes chemical preservatives are added to keep them longer. • Another form of vacuum packaging is Modified Atmosphere Packaging. The gas content within the packaging material is altered, i.e. the amount of oxygen is reduced and the amount of carbon dioxide is increased. This slows down the rate of food spoilage and aerobic bacteria cannot grow.	Cold meats, cheese, bacon, fish. Bacon and ready-prepared washed salads and salad leaves.

There are many other forms of preservation of foods such as salting, smoking, bottling and canning. You would not be asked a specific question about these methods in an examination.

Food poisoning

Food poisoning is an illness caused by the eating of contaminated or poisonous food.

Causes

Most causes of food poisoning are due to bacterial contamination of food, i.e. the food becomes contaminated with bacteria which then enter the digestive system and cause illness. It is very difficult to detect if food has become infected with bacteria that can cause food poisoning. The food may be infected with bacteria but it may look, smell and taste normal. The types of bacteria that can cause illness are known as pathogenic bacteria.

Bacteria are generally only harmful if they are present in very large numbers in food. Some food may have been infected with bacteria for a long period of time and toxins (poisons) may have formed in the food before consumption. Other bacteria only produce the toxins once they have entered the digestive system.

Symptoms of food poisoning:

Food poisoning can be mild or severe. The symptoms will vary slightly, depending on what type of bacteria is responsible for the poisoning. General symptoms include:

- severe vomiting
- diarrhoea
- exhaustion
- headache
- fever
- abdominal pain
- tiredness.

If you think you have food poisoning you should seek medical attention. You should also avoid preparing or handling food, in case you transfer food poisoning bacteria on to other people.

We know that bacteria are one of the main causes of food poisoning. So how can we prevent it? There are a large number of steps that we can take to prevent food spoilage, food contamination and so food poisoning. These start when buying food and finish when we serve food.

Buying foods

Step to take	Reason for step
Do not buy food that has past its 'use by date'.	The food is perishable and may be contaminated with bacteria. It is illegal to sell food once it has reached its use by date.
Do not buy tinned food which is bashed, blown or rusted.	This means that the food has not been stored correctly and has potentially been contaminated.
Do not buy frozen food (e.g. vegetables) which have frozen together in the pack.	This indicates that the food has started to defrost at some stage. There is the potential for bacterial growth to have increased in this time. If the food has been refrozen, this means more dormant bacteria.
Ensure that packaging is always intact.	Where packaging is damaged, it may mean that food contamination has taken place.
Buy only from shops that are clean and hygienic.	Use your common sense. A shop that sells food and which looks unclean may not be the best place to buy from. Make sure the shop assistants observe good hygiene.

The Foundation and General papers sometimes have illustrations of situations that are unhygienic. Remember to look for all the personal and kitchen hygiene rules, as well as remembering the points made in this section.

Transporting food back to the home

Just as it is important to use your common sense when buying food, it is important to remember to use your common sense when packing food so as to prevent food contamination.

Step to take	Reason for step
Plan your shopping journey in advance.	If you are buying frozen foods, buy these last and only when you are ready to go home. You do not want to give the food time to start to defrost as bacteria may start to multiply.
Try to keep frozen and chilled foods cold.	Pack in the boot of the car – which may be the coldest part of the car. Use cool boxes where possible to keep food cold. Pack frozen and chilled foods together to maintain cold conditions.
Keep cooked and uncooked foods apart.	Bacteria may spread from uncooked to cooked foods, so keep them apart when packing the shopping.
Pack dry and moist foods separately.	This will prevent dry food products, or their packaging, from becoming damp.
Pack household chemicals away from food.	This will prevent any chemical contamination of food and prevent chemical odours tainting food.

Storing food in the home

Correct storage of food in the home is essential if food contamination is to be prevented. There are many simple rules that should be followed to ensure that food stays fresh for as long as possible.

Step to take	Reason for step
Unpack food as quickly as possible – especially perishable foods.	Perishable and frozen foods should be placed into chilled conditions as quickly as possible to ensure that bacterial growth is not assisted.
Use up old stocks of food before buying new ones.	This ensures that food does not reach its expiry date. Throw out food that is out of date – the quality of the food cannot be guaranteed.
Keep dry food in cool, dry, clean places.	This ensures that food remains in good condition and prevents contamination from other sources.

Cross-contamination of food

We have seen that bacteria can contaminate food. The main carriers of contamination are shown below:

Human beings: Bacteria are found on our bodies – our hair, hands, mouth, nose, ears, and intestines all contain bacteria. When we sneeze, cough, spit and blow our nose, we are spreading bacteria. Care must be taken when working with food.

Pets and other animals: pets and other animals such as flies, mice and rats are all carriers of bacteria – some of which are pathogenic. Animals should be kept out of food preparation areas.

Rubbish: rubbish attracts all types of animals – from flies to stray cats and dogs. If rubbish is stored in or near food preparation areas, the risk of bacterial contamination of food is increased. Rubbish also contains lots of bacteria, which can be spread to food.

Food: raw food may come into the home contaminated with bacteria. If stored correctly and cooked correctly, this should not cause problems.

Cross-contamination is the process by which bacteria are transferred from one area to another. All of the above are potential vehicles for cross-contamination. This is a major cause of food contamination and food poisoning. By following simple rules, cross-contamination can be prevented:

Cooked and raw foods must always be stored apart.	→	Bacteria can spread from the raw food to the cooked food.
Use separate equipment for raw foods and cooked foods – or wash thoroughly before use.	→	Bacteria can spread from the raw food to the equipment being used. If not cleaned properly, cross-contamination occurs.
Wash all work surfaces thoroughly after preparing raw foods.	→	This will eliminate the risk of cross-contamination, particularly if hot water and a detergent are used.
Hands should be washed thoroughly after handling raw foods.	→	This will eliminate the risk of cross-contamination, particularly if hot water and a detergent are used.
Wooden chopping boards, wooden spoons and cracked crockery should not be used if possible.	→	Wooden chopping boards, wooden spoons and cracked crockery may all harbour bacteria.
Cleaning cloths should be disinfected on a very regular basis – ideally use disposable cloths.	→	Wiping a chopping board after cutting raw meat means that bacteria have crossed over to the cloth. This in turn can contaminate other areas.
Food should be covered at all stages of production.	→	This prevents cross-contamination from animals such as flies.

Common food poisoning situations

Frozen turkey needs to be defrosted fully before cooking. If not, the centre of the food does not cook to a high enough temperature to kill pathogenic (disease-producing) bacteria present. The middle of the turkey will be nice and warm and bacteria will grow and multiply. Your Christmas present from the bacteria will be food poisoning.

Foods that are being cooked and then used at a later date need careful handling. Once cooked, the food should be cooled rapidly, then stored and covered in a refrigerator until required. Food, which is left to sit on a work surface to cool, will attract pests such as flies. The food will also be in the danger zone of between 5°C to 63°C for a long period of time, allowing bacterial growth if the food has been contaminated.

It is very important that the food is **reheated** to at least a core temperature of 82°C to destroy bacteria. Food should never be reheated on more than one occasion.

Cooked rice can be very dangerous if it has not been cooled quickly and then reheated to the correct temperature. Rice contains a bacterium that can produce spores and toxins. It is better if rice is cooked as and when required.

The centre of food should normally reach 75°C to ensure food safety. Foods that are being reheated should reach a temperature of 82°C. Foods that have been cooked and are to be sold have to be held at a temperature of at least 63°C.

Food labelling and food hygiene

There are specific labelling requirements, which are in place to help prevent poor food storage and so prevent food spoilage and food poisoning.

Date marking

We already know that we cannot always tell if food is 'off' simply by looking at and smelling the food. For this reason, a 'Use By' date mark on food is important.

USE BY
12 MAR

The Use By date is found on products that are highly perishable, such as meat products, cream, yoghurts and ready meals. This means that the food must be used by the date given. If the food is consumed after this date, health can be put at risk. These products are usually high-risk foods, i.e. foods that can provide ideal growing conditions for bacteria. It is against the law for a retailer to sell or display food for sale which has gone past its Use By date. It is important to remember that the Use By date only applies to the condition of the food when purchased, i.e. if the food was frozen or cooked once purchased this would extend its life.

BEST BEFORE
16 Nov 2002

The 'Best Before' date is found on products that are less perishable. This label means that the product is at its best (in terms of quality, flavour and texture) before the date shown. The food may still be consumed after this date, but it may not be at its best quality.

Food manufacturers also provide other information that can be very useful in trying to prevent food spoilage and food poisoning.

Food labels have to provide instructions for safe storage. These are quite important as the Use By and Best Before dates are based on the consumer using the correct storage conditions for the product.

STORAGE INSTRUCTIONS	STORAGE INSTRUCTIONS	STORAGE INSTRUCTIONS
Store out of direct sunshine.	**Once opened, store in refrigerator.**	**Store in refrigerator after opening. Eat within three days of opening.**
Instructions found on a bottle of lemonade.	Instructions found on mayonnaise.	Instructions found on a carton of ready-made custard.

Manufacturers also have to provide directions to ensure the safe preparation or cooking of the food. If food has to be cooked, then accurate instructions have to be given to ensure that the food can be cooked correctly and so prevent food poisoning.

BEST COOKED FROM FROZEN

Place in a pre-heated oven at 200°C, Gas mark 6 for 1 hour and 10 minutes.

Ensure the product is piping hot before serving.

Instructions for cooking a pre-prepared chicken pie.

We often buy frozen food and it is important that we store it correctly to prevent food spoilage. Food labels also provide guidance to help consumers store these foods correctly.

Frozen food can be stored in the icebox of a refrigerator.

STORAGE INSTRUCTIONS

PRODUCE STORED IN	CONSUME WITHIN
Main compartment of refrigerator or cool place	24 hours of purchase
[*] frozen food compartment	1 week of purchase
[**] frozen food compartment	1 month of purchase
[***] frozen food compartment	3 months of purchase
[*|***] Food freezer	3 months of purchase

DO NOT REFREEZE AFTER THAWING

[*|***] Both frozen and fresh foods can be stored in a freezer for a maximum of three months.

[*] Frozen food can only be stored for a maximum of one week.

[**] Frozen food can only be stored for a maximum of one month.

[***] Frozen food can only be stored for a maximum of three months.

Food must not be refrozen once defrosted. Bacterial multiplication will have increased once the product has thawed.

The star rating can be found on all domestic refrigerators which have an ice box compartment.

[***] If the ice box has a three star rating the product can be stored for a maximum of three months. One, two and three star rated refrigerators will not have ice boxes at a sufficiently low enough temperature to make bacteria dormant. They will still be able to grow slowly. The higher the star rating, the lower the temperature the icebox can reach.

Refrigerators and freezers

Refrigerators and freezers have an important role in the prevention of food spoilage and food poisoning. In both refrigerators and freezers, temperature is reduced and so bacterial growth is reduced. It is important, however, that both the refrigerator and the freezer are used correctly to prevent food spoilage and food poisoning.

Use of refrigerators

A refrigerator normally has an internal temperature of between 2°C and 4°C. This is sufficiently cold to reduce bacterial growth, but not stop it. For this reason, refrigeration is only a short-term storage measure. Some refrigerators have an icebox. This is the coldest part of the fridge, and is normally marked with a star rating (see previous page). There are, however, a number of important rules that should be followed to ensure the safe storage of food within the refrigerator.

Rule	Comments
Ensure the refrigerator is working at a temperature between 2°C and 4°C.  	Use a refrigerator thermometer to ensure that the interior of the refrigerator is working at this temperature. Do not place hot food in the interior of the refrigerator – cool it first. Placing hot food in the refrigerator will increase the temperature above 4°C and bacterial growth will increase. Do not leave the refrigerator door open for long periods of time as this will increase the temperature of the fridge above 4°C.
Do not overload the refrigerator.	Cold air needs to circulate around the food which is stored inside the fridge. This cannot happen if the refrigerator is overfilled.
Store food correctly in the refrigerator.  	Cooked and raw food should be stored in different areas of the refrigerator to prevent cross contamination. Raw food should be stored below cooked food to prevent cross-contamination. All food should be covered, not only to prevent cross-contamination but also to prevent moisture loss. Ensure that all food is removed from the refrigerator when it has reached its date mark.
Regular maintenance of the refrigerator is important.	Keep the interior of the refrigerator clean, removing spills and food deposits whenever they occur. This will help prevent contamination of food. If the refrigerator needs to be defrosted, ensure that this is done on a regular basis – this will prevent a build up of ice on the icebox.

Use of freezers

A freezer normally has an internal temperature of –18°C or below. This is cold enough to stop bacterial growth. For this reason, freezing food is suitable for both short and longer term food storage.

Some freezers have a quick freeze facility where the internal temperature of the freezer can be reduced to –24°C.

Most food contains large amounts of water. When water is frozen, ice is formed. Large ice crystals are formed when food is frozen slowly. This can damage the cell structure of the food. When the food defrosts, the water enclosed within the cells is released. The food can appear to look 'soggy'.

At lower temperatures, smaller ice crystals form so the damage to the cell structure is reduced. Therefore, when the food is defrosted, it keeps its shape better.

There are, however, a number of important rules that should be followed to ensure the safe storage of food within the freezer.

Rule	Comments
Ensure the freezer is working at a temperature below –18°C.	Use a freezer thermometer to ensure that the interior of the freezer is working at this temperature. Do not place hot food in the interior of the freezer – cool it first. Placing hot food in the freezer will increase the temperature and bacterial growth will increase. Do not leave the freezer door open for long periods of time, as this will increase the temperature of the freezer – particularly if the freezer is an upright freezer.
Do not overload the freezer.	Cold air needs to circulate around the food which is stored inside the freezer. This cannot happen if the freezer is overfilled.
Store food correctly in the freezer.	All food should be clearly marked showing its contents and date when frozen. This will allow you to take out the food you require, and allow you to throw out food that has been stored for too long. Wrap food well before freezing – otherwise the food will dry out. Only freeze food which is in its best condition – it will last for a longer period of time. Remove as much air from the food packaging as possible before freezing. This will help prevent the food drying out during storage.
Regular maintenance of the freezer is important.	Keep the interior of the freezer clean, removing spills and food deposits whenever they occur. This will help prevent contamination of food. Defrost the freezer on a regular basis.
Never refreeze defrosted food.	When the food is thawing, bacterial growth will increase. When you refreeze the food, you are freezing food with an increased number of bacteria present.

Safe working practices

Safe working practices

Every year, hundreds of people are killed or injured in the home as a result of accidents. Many of these accidents can be avoided by taking simple preventative measures. The main accidents that occur in the home are:

• cuts • burns • scalds • falls • electric shocks • poisoning.

Young children and elderly people are the two groups who are most at risk from accidents in the home. Young children tend to be curious and this can lead to accidents. Elderly people may become less able to react to situations as they happen and this can lead to accidents. This section is all about trying to prevent accidents before they occur.

Use of food preparation equipment

In the kitchen, we use a lot of food preparation equipment that can be dangerous if not used correctly.

Food preparation equipment	Procedures for safe use
Sharp utensils (e.g. knives) 	Sharp knives, scissors and skewers are a potential danger because of their sharp edges. They should never be left lying on a work surface in case young children can reach them. Knives should be kept in a knife block or drawer that can be locked. Scissors and skewers should be kept in an area children cannot access. Sharp utensils which have been used for food preparation should be placed in a safe area until they are ready to be cleaned. Leaving such objects in the sink can be dangerous.
Gas and electric cookers 	Gas appliances should always be fitted by a registered gas fitter. If a gas leak is suspected, TRANSCO should be immediately contacted. (TRANSCO is the body responsible for the delivery of gas to the home.) Cookers should not be placed next to windows if there is a danger of gas burners being blown out by draughts or if there are blinds or curtains nearby that might catch fire. Cookers should be switched off when not being used. Oven gloves should be used when taking items from the oven. Hob guards can be purchased to prevent young children gaining access to the hob area of the cooker. This can prevent young children pulling hot pans from the hob. Young children should not be allowed into the kitchen without supervision when the cooker is operating.
Electrical equipment 	Never handle electrical equipment with wet hands – this can lead to electrocution. Electrical equipment should always be switched off at the mains supply before and after use. Electrical equipment, such as food processors, should never be assembled or disassembled when plugged into the electricity supply. Never immerse electrical equipment into water or put it in a dishwasher. Never use electrical equipment that is damaged in any way. This includes a frayed flex or a damaged plug. Always check that the fuse used in the plug is the correct amp for the appliance. Always read instruction manuals before use.

Food preparation equipment	Procedures for safe use
Microwave oven	The use of a microwave oven to fry food is not recommended as there is no way to regulate the temperature of the fat/oil. Microwave cookers should be tested yearly for possible microwave leakage. Metal objects should not be placed in microwave ovens. This can lead to sparking which can damage the oven. When using clingfilm on products which are to be cooked in the microwave, use the non-PVC type which is safe for use in microwave ovens. Microwave containers can get very hot – remove them from the oven carefully and remove any lid or clingfilm covering the food with great care.

Care must be taken when using hot fat, oil and liquids. These cooking media are potentially dangerous because:

- they can reach a very high temperature
- when spilt they can cover a large section of the body very easily.

When cooking with hot fats and oils, a thermostatically controlled frying pan is the best option, as the pan will automatically cut off when the correct temperature has been reached. A pan of hot oil or fat must never be left unattended as it can quickly catch fire.

If a fat or oil fire occurs the following actions should be taken:

- Do not panic – keep calm.
- Switch off the gas burner or electric cooker ring.
- Place a damp cloth or fire blanket over the burning pan.
- Leave the pan to cool down.

You must NEVER:

- grab the pan and try to take it outside. The flames may blow onto your body. The oxygen in the air will feed the fire and again put you at further risk.
- throw water over the fire – this will cause the hot fat to spit and increase the vigour of the fire.

Care of clothing

When caring for clothing it is important that we follow safe practices when using items of equipment.

Laundering equipment	Procedures for safe use
Washing machine	Follow the general instructions listed on page 59 for the use of electrical equipment.  Do not leave detergents and other chemicals lying where young children have access to them. Ensure that any safety lock features on the washing machine are working. Read the manufacturer's instructions before use. Ensure that young children do not have access to the washing machine whilst it is operational – some wash programmes use very hot water.
Tumble-drier	Follow the general instructions listed on page 59 for the use of electrical equipment. 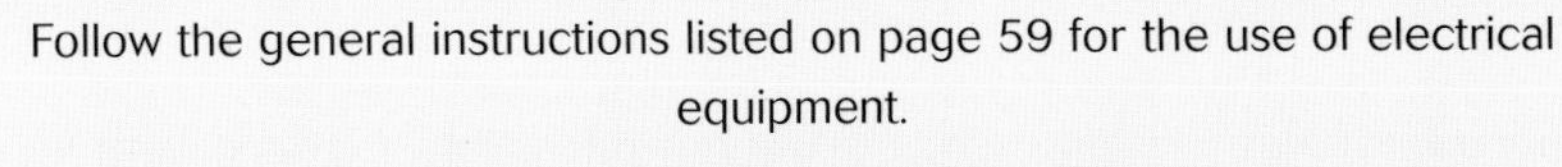 Ensure that any safety lock features on the tumble-drier are working. Read the manufacturer's instructions before use. Ensure that young children do not have access to the tumble-drier whilst it is operational.
Iron 	Follow the general instructions listed on page 59 for the use of electrical equipment. Read the manufacturer's instructions before use. Never leave an iron unattended – especially with young children in the home. If using a steam iron, only add water when the appliance is switched off. Rest the iron on its heel between ironing garments. Resting the iron on its sole plate can be dangerous. Leave the iron to cool down in a safe place (out of the reach of children) before storing the iron away. Always set the iron to the correct temperature for the type of fabric to be ironed.
Ironing board 	Use an ironing board that is level and steady when being used. This will prevent the iron from slipping or toppling off the ironing board. Store in a safe and secure place where it cannot topple over and cause an accident. Make sure that the ironing board cover is firmly secured with no loose ties that can attract a child's attention. Never leave an ironing board unattended when there are young children about.

Sewing equipment

When using sewing equipment there are a number of safety precautions that have to be considered.

Sewing equipment	Procedures for safe use
Pins and needles	Any pins or needles that are dropped on the ground should be picked up immediately. They may cause an accident to the foot or children may pick up and swallow them or otherwise injure themselves. Pins and needles should be stored in a safe container away from the reach of young children. Pins and needles are dangerous and should never be placed in the mouth or used as a play item for any reason.
Scissors	Scissors can pose potential danger because of their sharp edges and pointed end. They should never be left lying on a work surface in case young children can reach them. Scissors should be kept in a drawer that can be locked. When carrying scissors, hold them by the closed blades with the handle uppermost. When passing scissors to someone else, hold the closed blades in your hand and pass on to the other person with the handles uppermost.
Sewing machine	Follow the general instructions listed on page 59 for the use of electrical equipment. Only one person at a time should operate the sewing machine – it is very easy to lose your concentration and this can be dangerous. Hands and loose clothing should be kept well away from the moving needle. The sewing machine should be packed away after use and stored in an area where young children have no access. When packing the sewing machine away, ensure that the needle is at its lowest position – this prevents any accidents when unpacking. Care should be taken when lifting a sewing machine – it can cause back strain. The instruction manual must be read before operating the sewing machine. Regular maintenance is important to ensure that the sewing machine works correctly and safely.

Home safety

All of the safe practices listed above will help prevent accidents and ensure that the home is a safe place. There are many more safety precautions that can be taken throughout the home. Most of these are common-sense measures. No matter how safe you make your home, the chances are that there will still be some accidents. In an examination you would generally be asked to identify the main causes of accidents in the home and then give measures that you would take to prevent such accidents happening. In the chart below you will find some common types of hazards which can be found in the home (and which feature quite often in examination questions). The chart gives you the types of accident that can occur and some suggestions as to how the accident could be prevented.

Hazard	Type of Accident	Precaution
Sharp objects (e.g. scissors, knives, pins) lying on work areas	Cut	Remove to a safe area out of the reach of children. Remove to a locked drawer/cupboard.
Broken glass/crockery on the floor or on a worktop	Cut	Remove from the area, wrap in lots of newspaper and dispose of safely.

Hazard	Type of Accident	Precaution
Open coal fire in a room A burn is caused by dry heat	Burn	Do not light the fire unless there is adult supervision in the room. Place a fireguard round an open fire to prevent access to the fire by young children and to prevent sparks landing on carpets.
Matches/lighter left lying on a work area	Burn	Store matches/lighter in an area where young children cannot gain access.
Naked flames and heat generating equipment in the kitchen	Burn	Do not let young children into the kitchen unless supervised.
Mirror, banners, pictures over the fireplace	Burn	Do not place items which will be of interest to young children over or near the fireplace.
Fireworks/other flammable materials left lying in a garden/cupboard	Burn	Move to an area where children do not have access – preferably in a locked drawer or cupboard.
Removing foods from an oven using a teacloth/towel	Burn	Use oven gloves which are designed to provide an insulating layer between the hands and the hot dish.
Saucepans on the cooker hob with pan handles sticking out A scald is caused by hot liquid/steam	Scald	Turn the pan handles to the back or the sides of the cooker hob. Never allow children in the kitchen unsupervised. Use a cooker guard on the hob to prevent pans being toppled over.
Hot drinks, teapots lying on tables/work area	Scald	Do not leave hot drinks on tables, especially tables with tablecloths. A young child could pull the tablecloth and the hot drinks off the table.
Stairway/hall dimly lit	Fall	Ensure that stairways and other dimly lit areas have sufficient lighting to ensure good visibility.
Objects (e.g. toys, books, trailing flex) left lying	Fall	Tidy away all objects after use. Shorten flex lengths to prevent them trailing.
Rug placed on a polished floor	Fall	Do not place a rug on a highly polished floor unless it can be firmly secured in place.
Spills on the floor	Fall	Wipe up all spills immediately – especially if on a floor surface that could become slippery.
Babies/young children climbing stairs/entering the kitchen	Fall	Safety gates should be used to prevent babies and young children entering areas that can be dangerous.
Person using a stool to reach a high cupboard	Fall	Step ladders should be used to reach high areas as chairs and tables may collapse under the weight of a person. They may also be wobbly.
Using electrical equipment with wet hands	Electric shock	Only use electrical equipment with dry hands. Do not operate on/off switches with wet hands. Do not operate electrical equipment in the bathroom.
Overloaded power switches/adapters	Electric shock	Never overload power sockets.
Frayed flex on electrical equipment	Electric shock	Frayed flexes must always be repaired/replaced. Do not use the appliance until repaired.

Hazard	Type of Accident	Precaution
Child sticking fingers into electric socket	Electric shock	Use electric socket guards when there are young children in the house.
Medicines, chemicals, alcohol, etc, left lying on work areas	Poisoning	All medicines should be kept in a special cabinet out of the reach of young children. Chemicals and alcohol should be kept in areas which children cannot access.
Cleaning fluids kept in lemonade bottles	Poisoning	Always label chemicals clearly. Chemicals should be kept in areas which children cannot access.

Design features

Influences on choice of materials and resources

Design

Conservation of resources →

Influences on choice of materials and resources

There are a number of important considerations that we have to think about before buying goods and services. We all have different ideas about things that we like and dislike; we all have our favourite colours and our favourite foods. We take these into consideration when we buy goods and services.

In your question paper, you need to think about the factors that influence the choice of materials and equipment:

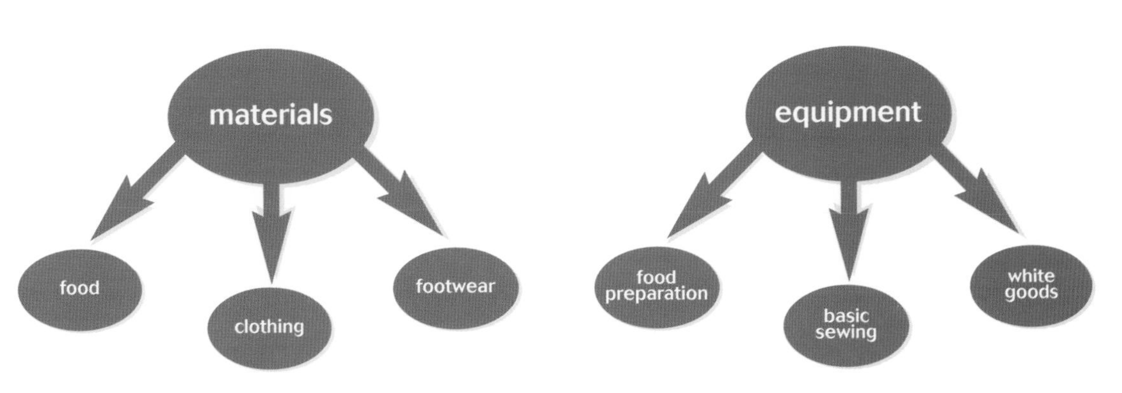

White goods are large items of electrical equipment such as cookers, washing machines and tumble-driers

Whatever the choice of item, there are a number of influences that will be considered before purchase.

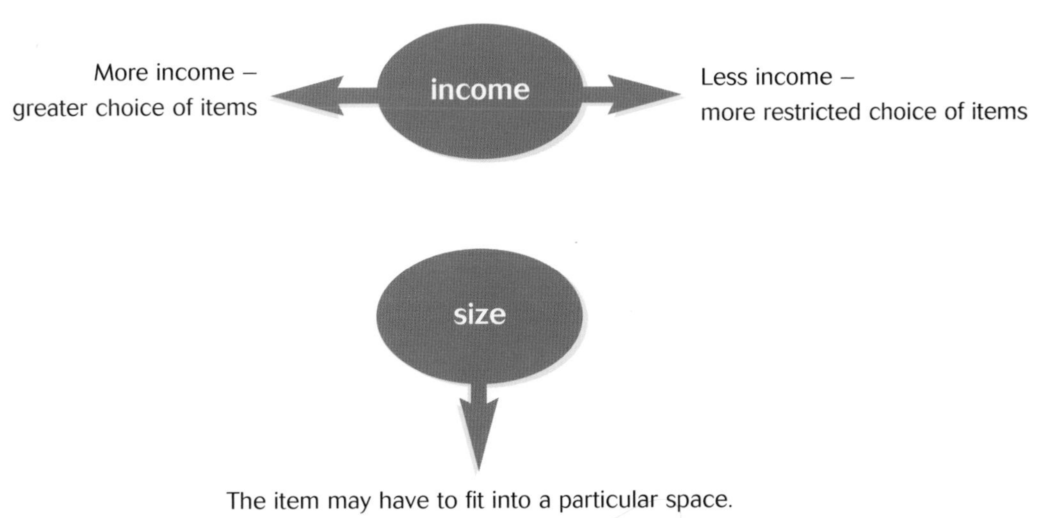

The item may have to fit into a particular space.

If you wear size 4 shoes, then you are limited to what is available in your size.

If you need to buy a cooker to fit into a particular space in the kitchen then you are limited to what is available to fit that space.

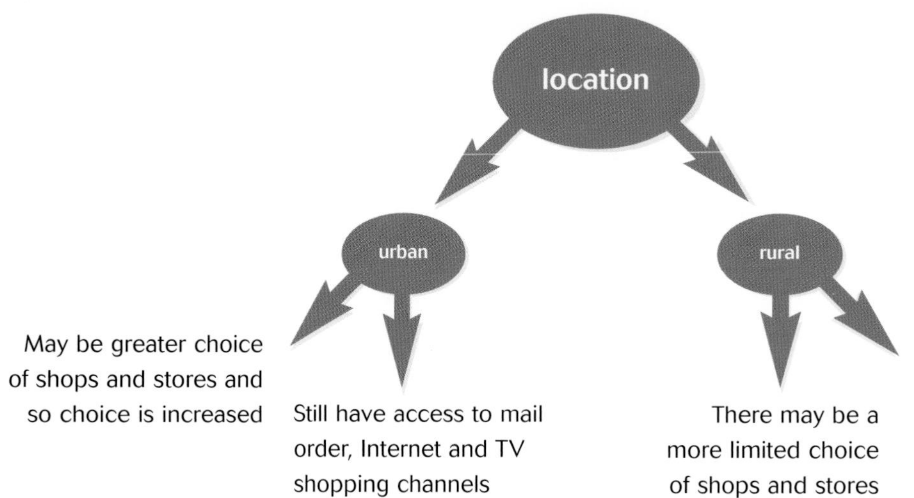

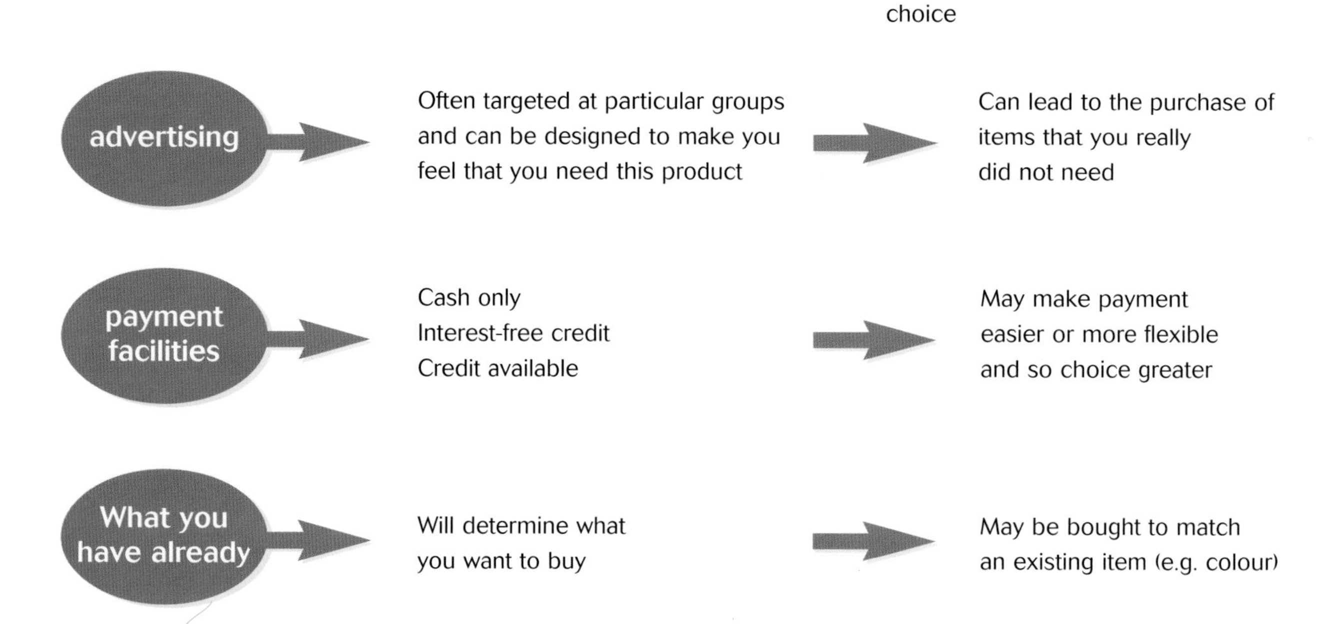

Whenever you decide to buy a particular product, there may be a wide selection available to you, even if you have limited funds.

In such cases, you will have to look at the types of design features available on each of the different products, and then decide which of these are the most important to you. Here is an example:

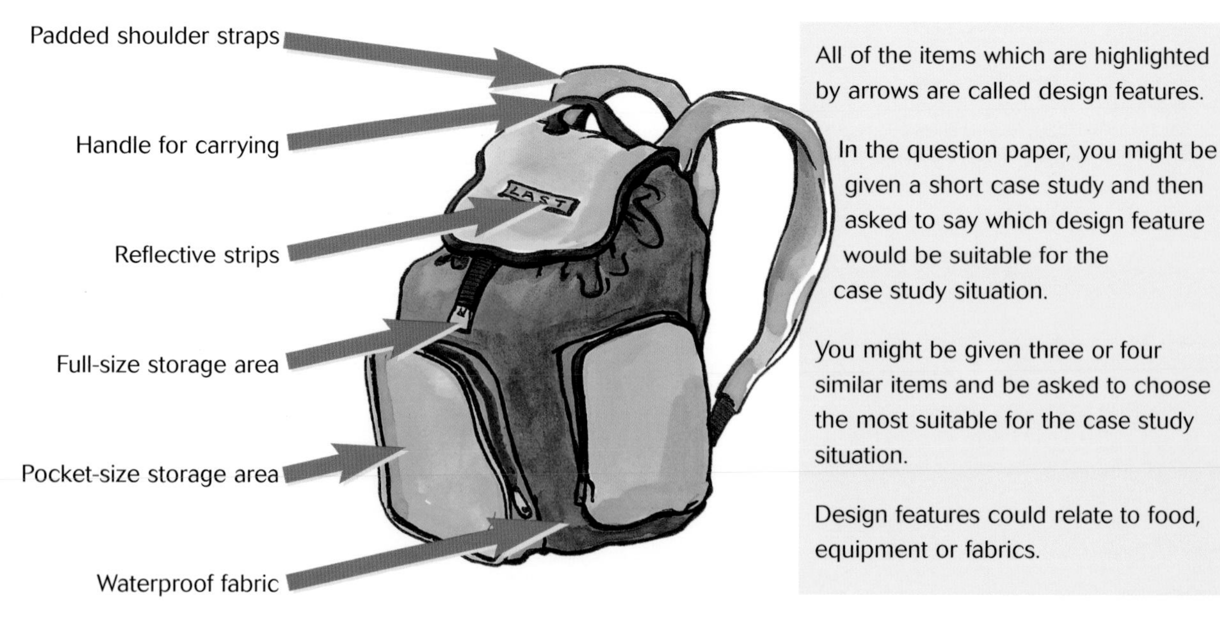

All of the items which are highlighted by arrows are called design features.

In the question paper, you might be given a short case study and then asked to say which design feature would be suitable for the case study situation.

You might be given three or four similar items and be asked to choose the most suitable for the case study situation.

Design features could relate to food, equipment or fabrics.

If I wanted the backpack to be brightly coloured, and it is only made in black, this might not be the best choice for me. I would then need to look at other types and designs until I found the one that met all my needs. What I am looking at are all the design features that will make the backpack suitable for me.

Design

When a designer is designing a product, he or she will have to think not only about the design features, but also about what the item is going to be used for, i.e. he or she will have to design the item to make sure that it is fit for its purpose.

When thinking about the design of an item, there are a number of different areas that a designer will have to think about:

- Materials to be used — are they suitable for the item?
- Construction — are the best methods of construction being used?
- Performance — does the item do what it is meant to?
- Safety — will the item be safe to use?
- Durability — will the item last for a reasonable time?
- Aesthetic properties — does the item look good?

These areas have to be considered, no matter what the item being designed is – whether it is a food product, a textile product, or an item of equipment.

Let's look at some different products and discuss how each of the design areas listed above is important.

Product 1: Low-fat ready-to-eat custard

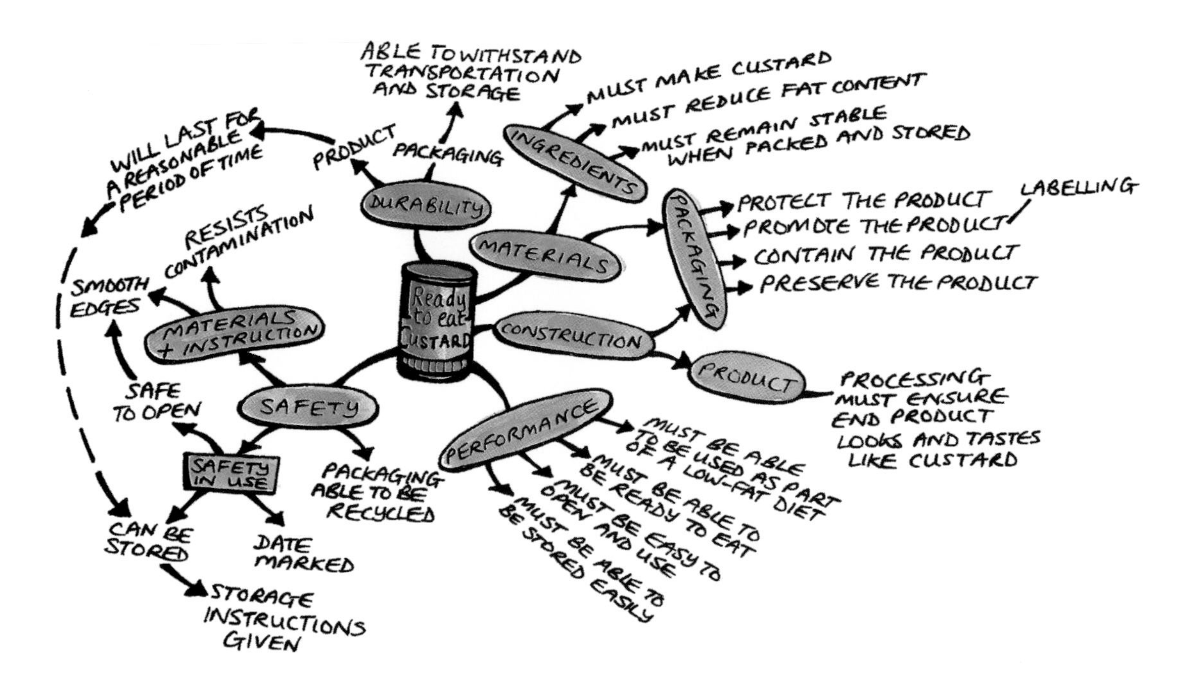

As well as the above factors, the consumer would also consider the following – all of which will vary from person to person:

Appearance	Does the product look nice? Will I be tempted to buy it and eat it?
Colour	Does the colour look nice and encourage me to eat the product? Does the colour of the product reflect its name (e.g. strawberry flavour custard should not be yellow)?
Fashionable	Some foods become fashionable and are popular with different groups. Some sports drinks have become fashionable, so people buy them for this reason.
Likes and dislikes	You will only buy food that you know will be liked and used by your family.
Family and peer pressure	There may be a reluctance to buy certain types of food if it has never been tried before. You may decide to eat certain products (e.g. vegetarian food) because your friends are doing this.
Personal and family beliefs and values	There may be religious, cultural and moral reasons for not choosing certain food.

Product 2: Textile items

When talking about materials to be used for textile items, it is important to know that different fibres have different properties. When fibres are used to make fabrics, the types and quantities of fibres combined together will give the end product different properties.

The chart overleaf summarises the main properties of different types of fibres.

When making textile items, the designer has to think about the properties that an item will need. Here is a list of fabric properties:

Properties	Description
Strength	How strong the fabric is – is it made with a strong fibre or a weak and delicate fibre?
Durability	How hard wearing the fabric is – can it take a lot of rubbing, washing, ironing for example?
Ease of laundering	How easily can the fabric be cared for? Can it be machine washed or does it have to be dry cleaned?
Absorbency	How much moisture can the fabric absorb?
Stain resistance	How resistant the fabric is to staining – some fabrics can be treated to make them stain resistant.
Crease resistance	How well the fabric resists creasing – both when wearing and when laundering. .
Flammability	How flame resistant the fabric is – some fabrics can be specially treated.
Water repellence	The ability to prevent the absorption of water
Elasticity	The ability of the fabric to stretch
Breathability	The ability to let moisture out, but not let water in
Insulation/warmth	The ability to keep warmth around the body

Different items require different properties:

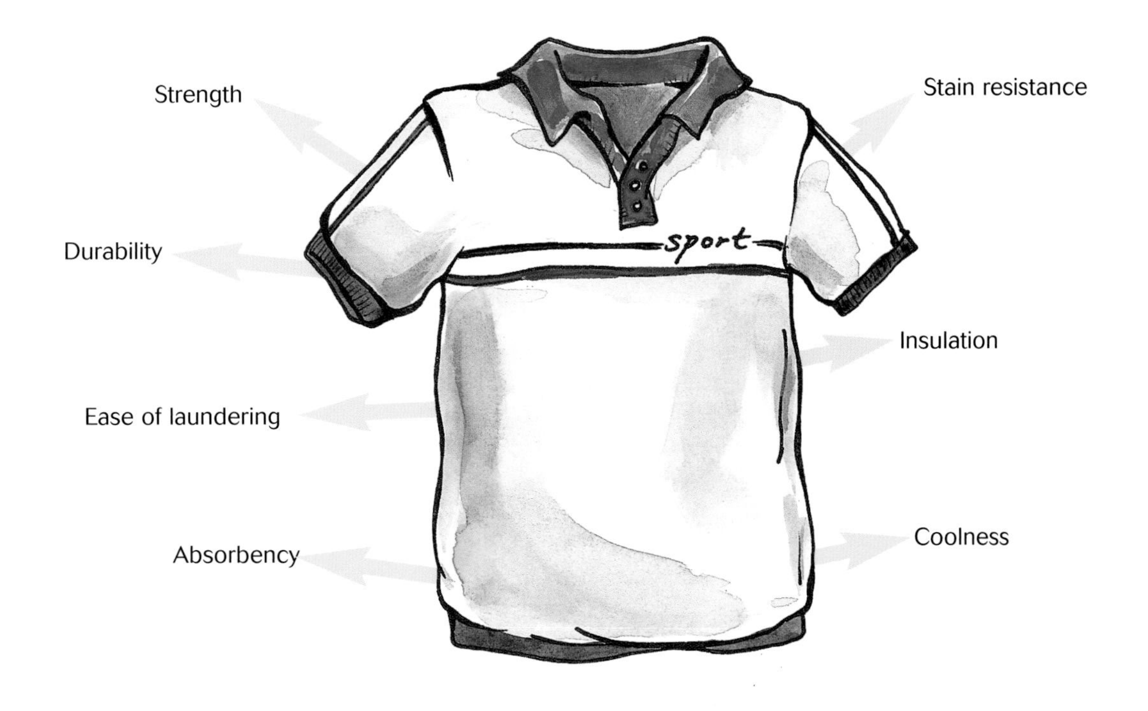

A jacket used for hillwalking would require different properties:

All of these properties will be determined by the properties of the materials that the designer used when planning the product. This may involve the use of only one fibre type, or a combination of others.

Fibre type / Property	Absorbency	Durability	Strength	Warmth	Resistance to creasing	Elasticity	Flame resistance	Ease of washing
Cotton	*****	*****	****	**	*	***	*	****
Linen	*****	*****	*****	***	*	*	*	**
Silk	*****	*****	****	****	**	***	***	*
Wool	*****	*	*	*****	*****	*****	***	*
Acrylic	***	***	****	*****	*****	*****	*	****
Polyester	*	*****	*****	**	*****	***	****	****
Nylon	*	*****	*****	*	****	*****	****	****
Viscose	*****	*	***	*	*	*	*	***
Acetate	****	*	***	*	***	***	***	***
Elastane	*	*****	****	**	*****	*****	*	****

* = poor   ***** = good

Elastane is a stretchy fibre made from a substance called polyurethane.

Cotton, wool, silk and linen are all natural fibres.

Polyester, nylon, rayon, viscose, acetate and elastane are classified as synthetic fibres or man made fibres.

Different fibres can be combined together to improve the overall performance of a fabric. For example, polyester and cotton are often combined and used in the production of fabric for shirts and blouses. Polyester brings the fabric some of the properties, such as crease-resistance, that cotton lacks. Cotton provides properties, such as absorbency and warmth, that polyester lacks.

Fabric can have special finishes added to them in order to improve their performance. Here are some examples:

- **Flameproof finish** – added to cotton and linen for furnishing fabrics
- **Waterproof finish** – added to cotton, wool, silk and linen for clothing
- **Stain resistant finish** – can be added to most fabrics
- **Shrink resistant finish** – can be added to cotton and wool for clothing
- **Antistatic finish** – can be added to nylon and polyester used for underwear.

Special fabrics have now been designed that incorporate specially developed fibres, which can be used to make lightweight fabrics and have a variety of uses. One example is Trevira Finesse – a polyester fabric. It is made from very fine fibres which are lightly woven together, leaving the fabric with very small pores. This prevents the fabric from becoming wet, whilst still allowing vapour from perspiration to pass through.

Gore-Tex: A special membrane which consists of millions of tiny holes, small enough to keep rain out but large enough to let water vapour from perspiration out. This makes the membrane especially suitable for use in sportswear.

Product 3: Child's goalkeeper top

Appearance	Does the product look good? Does it resemble a goalkeeper top? Will I be tempted to buy it and wear it?
Colour	Does the colour look good and encourage me to buy the product? Are there a variety of colours available so that I can buy one that matches my favourite team? Does the item have to co-ordinate with other items I have (e.g. football shorts)?
Fashionable	Is the product fashionable and something that I want to wear? Many teenagers and young people are keen to wear what are considered the most fashionable 'labels', i.e. designer clothing.
Likes and dislikes	We all have personal likes and dislikes. If you do not like the look or colour of the product, you will have to keep on looking around different shops.
Family and peer pressure	In some households, parents buy clothes for their children; their taste in what is acceptable or not may differ from their children's. This may be a purchase to 'be like your friends' if they have similar tops.
Personal and family beliefs and values	Certain religions and cultures have special rules about clothing. Some families may not buy clothing if it has been made in countries where children may have been forced to work in slave labour conditions to manufacture them.

Conservation of resources

The conservation of resources is an additional factor that many people take into account when considering the choice of materials and equipment. In particular, there are two main areas to be considered:

- conservation of energy/running costs
- recycled/recyclable goods.

Conservation of energy and reduction of running costs

Conservation of energy is all about trying to reduce the amount of energy that you use in the home. This also includes choosing electrical equipment that uses energy wisely and has low running costs. There are some simple rules that you can follow to save energy in different parts of the home.

- If your boiler is more than 15 years old it will be less efficient than a modern one. Modern boilers use less fuel to produce the same amount of heat. Replacing an old boiler could save you a fifth off your fuel bills.
- 20% of heat can be lost through draughty, ill-fitting doors and windows.
- Double glazing cuts heat loss with the help of air trapped in the gap between the two panes of glass. This air doesn't mix with the air in the room or that outside, so creating an insulating barrier. This also reduces noise and condensation problems.
- Draughts enter your home in gaps around doors; windows and floors, accounting for up to 20% of lost heat. Wherever you can feel cold air coming in, warm air is going out. Draft exclusion strips can be placed around draughty windows and doors.
- Loft insulation that is 20cm thick can cut 20% off heating bills.
- Walls lose more heat than any other part of your home – consider cavity wall insulation.
- Ordinary light bulbs use up to four times as much electricity as energy-saving alternatives. Energy-saving light bulbs use electronics that enable them to produce light using a fraction of the energy.
- Reducing your heating thermostat by 1°C can cut up to 10% off fuel bills.
- For every minute that a fridge door is open, it will take 3 minutes for it to regain its temperature.
- A new energy efficient fridge/freezer could reduce the amount of electricity used by up to 50%.
- A shower uses only two-fifths of the water needed for a bath.
- By insulating your hot water tank and pipes, you will retain hot water for longer, and save money on heating it. Insulate pipes if you can – especially between the boiler and the hot water cylinder if you have one.
- The technology used in new washing and drying appliances means that they use less water and electricity.

Some simple tips that can also help save energy:

- Always remember to turn off the lights when you leave a room.
- Always remember to put the plug in a basin or sink. Leaving hot water taps running without the plug in is wasteful.
- Choose the right size pan for the food and cooker, and keep lids on when cooking. Don't use any more water than you need.
- Don't overfill the kettle; just heat the amount of water you really need – the kettle will boil more quickly.
- When using the washing machine wait until you have a full load before using, or use the half load or economy programme if your machine has one.
- Most modern washing powders work effectively at lower temperatures, so unless you have very dirty clothes to wash, try using the low temperature programme.
- If you have a tumble-drier, avoid filling it with really wet clothes – wring them out or spin-dry them first.
- With dishwashers, try using a low-temperature programme unless there are some really dirty dishes to tackle.
- Close your curtains in the evening to stop heat escaping through the windows.
- If you are going away for a few days, leave the thermostat on a low setting to provide protection from freezing without costing too much.

For more information on how to save energy in the home, visit the following web site:

http://www.est.org.uk/

When we are purchasing equipment, there are a number of actions that we can take to ensure we are buying equipment which will conserve energy and reduce running costs. In particular there are a number of design features built into modern appliances that will help to conserve energy.

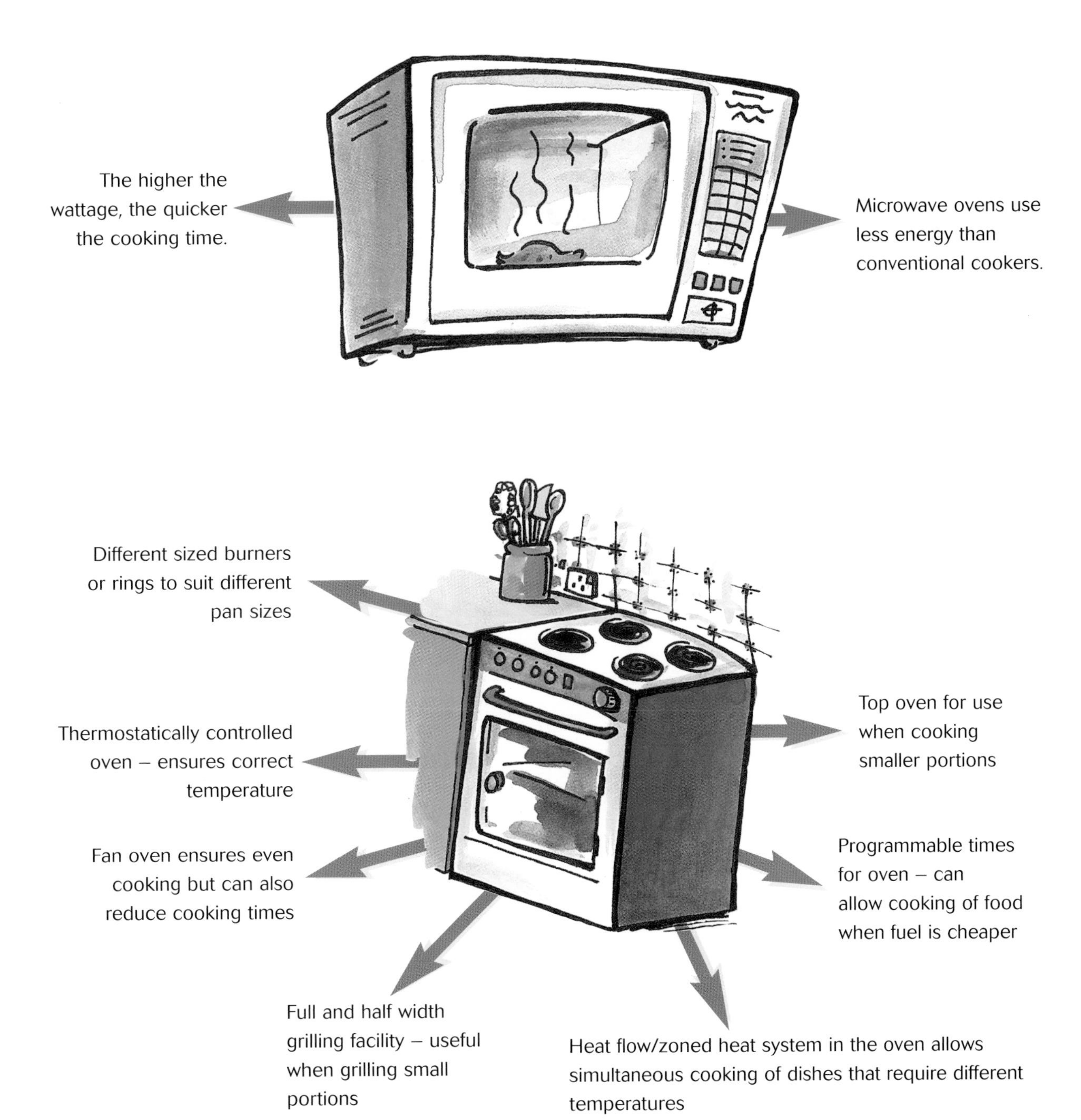

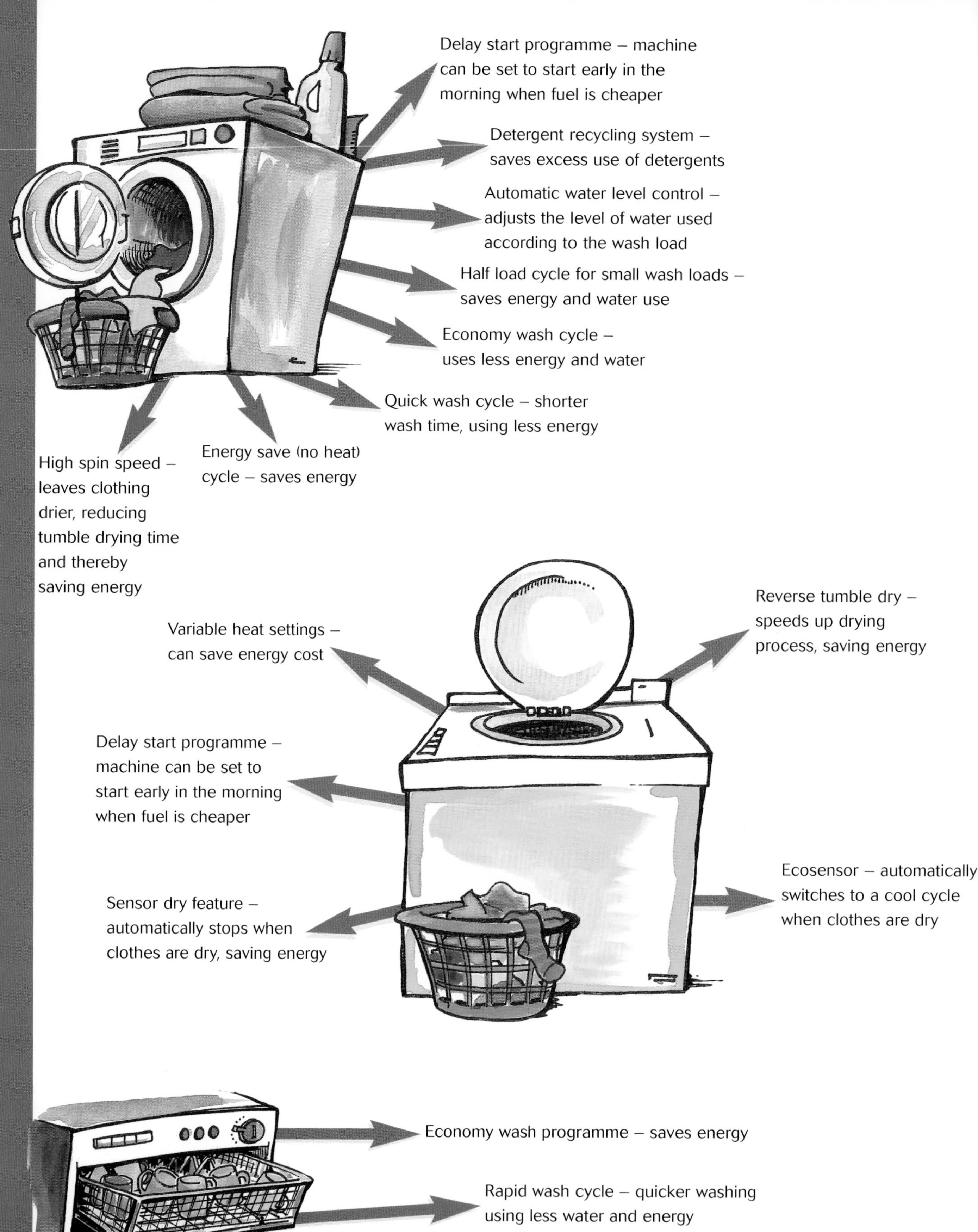
Delay start programme – machine can be set to start early in the morning when fuel is cheaper
Detergent recycling system – saves excess use of detergents
Automatic water level control – adjusts the level of water used according to the wash load
Half load cycle for small wash loads – saves energy and water use
Economy wash cycle – uses less energy and water
Quick wash cycle – shorter wash time, using less energy
High spin speed – leaves clothing drier, reducing tumble drying time and thereby saving energy
Energy save (no heat) cycle – saves energy
Variable heat settings – can save energy cost
Reverse tumble dry – speeds up drying process, saving energy
Delay start programme – machine can be set to start early in the morning when fuel is cheaper
Ecosensor – automatically switches to a cool cycle when clothes are dry
Sensor dry feature – automatically stops when clothes are dry, saving energy

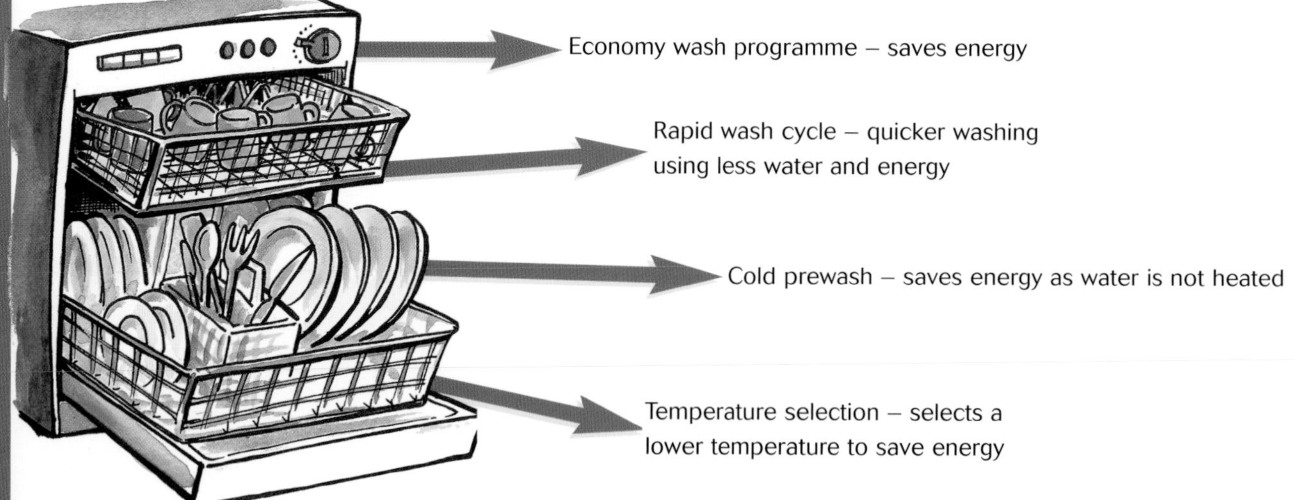
Economy wash programme – saves energy
Rapid wash cycle – quicker washing using less water and energy
Cold prewash – saves energy as water is not heated
Temperature selection – selects a lower temperature to save energy

Many appliances now have energy rating systems that can be used by consumers to choose between similar products.

The Energy Labelling Directive requires that appliances be labelled to show their power consumption in such a way that it is possible to compare the efficiency with that of other makes and models. The intention is that consumers will prefer more energy-efficient appliances to those with a higher consumption. The Directive covers the following appliances:

- washing machines
- electric tumble-driers
- refrigerators and freezers
- combined washer-driers
- dishwashers
- light bulbs.

The scheme labels products according to the amount of energy they use.
Products are rated on a 7-point scale:

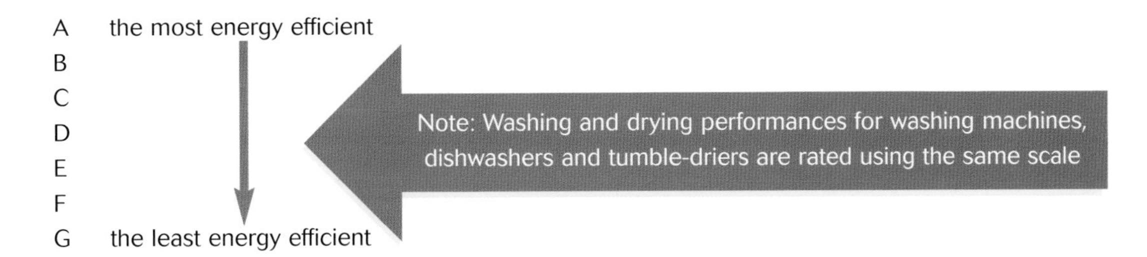

In addition, appliance labels now give a more detailed breakdown of their performance. Here are some examples showing the detail that is provided:

From a Washing Machine	
Energy Efficiency	Class A
Energy Consumption	0·95kWH/cycle
Washing Performance	A
Spin Drying Performance	C
Max. Spin Speed	1000RPM
Capacity (Cotton)	5kg (11lbs)
Water Consumption	59 litres
Estimated Annual Consumption:	
	Energy: 190kWH/year
	Water: 11800 litres

From a Fridge	
Energy Efficiency	Class C
Energy Consumption	347kWH/year

From a Fridge Freezer	
Energy Efficiency	Class A
Energy Consumption	365kWH/year

From a Dishwasher	
Energy Efficiency	Class D
Energy Consumption	1·6kWH/cycle
Washing Performance	B
Drying Performance	C
Water Consumption	19 litres

All these facts and figures can be good for the consumer, as they can make valid comparisons between similar products and select the products that best suit their needs.

Recycling is the process of recovering and reusing waste products – from household use, manufacturing, agriculture and business – thereby reducing the burden on the environment.

Many people are concerned about making good use of the resources that we have available and, where possible, trying not to waste these. Recycling and the use of recycled products is now big business and an area that is again being used by consumers when they are considering the choice of materials and resources.

Products that are recycled in large quantities include paper and paperboard, ferrous metals, aluminium and other non-ferrous metals, glass, plastics, and food waste.

Recycling Textiles

There are a number of steps that can be taken to recycle textiles – rather than just throw them away:

- Take them to a recycling centre where they can be used in a variety of ways, including making new fabrics.
- Take clothing and other textile items to a charity shop where they can be resold.
- Take clothing and blankets to charities who redistribute clothing at home and abroad.
- Old clothes can be cut up and used for patchwork or appliqué.
- Buttons, zips and trimmings can be removed and reused.

Recycling Other Household Products

Item	Ways to Recycle
Glass	Can be taken to a bottle bank so it is recycled. Bottles and jars can be used for storage of foods or other items.
Paper	Can be taken to a paper bank where it can be recycled.
Steel Cans	(Most food cans) These can be taken to special steel can banks for recycling.
Aluminium	(Most drink cans) These can be taken to aluminium banks where they can be recycled to make new cans. Many schools and offices have special recycling boxes for aluminium cans.
Plastics	Some plastics can be recycled, but all the different types of plastic need to be separated. Symbols are now found on plastic packaging materials to allow for the separation of different types of plastic. There tends to be fewer collection facilities for plastic materials. Plastic carrier bags can be reused. Plastic pots and bottles can be used to make craft items.
Food Waste	Food waste can be used in a compost heap.

As an alternative, consumers can look at the labels of products they are considering buying.

Most products will give an indication if they

- have used recycled materials when making their products;
- can be recycled once used.

These are symbols that can be found on the packaging of materials that can be recycled:

This symbol can be found on the base of plastic milk bottles.
The number and coding can be used to sort different types of plastic for recycling purposes.

This carton is made from 80% Recycled board RECYCLABLE

This symbol can be found on the packaging of a breakfast cereal box.

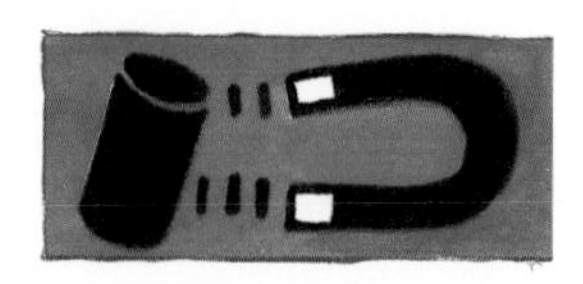

This symbol can be found on food cans. It means that this can is made from steel and can be recycled.

There are a variety of other environmental labelling schemes that can be found on food labels. These labels are explained on page 93 of this book.

Physical needs of individuals and families

Clothing

Shelter

Reliable sources of consumer advice

Consumer rights and responsibilities

Labelling of products

General wellbeing ➜

Clothing

We are all individuals who have different needs and wants. Just as we all look different, we all have different physical needs. In previous sections we have looked at the food needs of individuals and families. We all have different needs for clothing as well and this is what we will look at in this section.

Why do we need clothing?

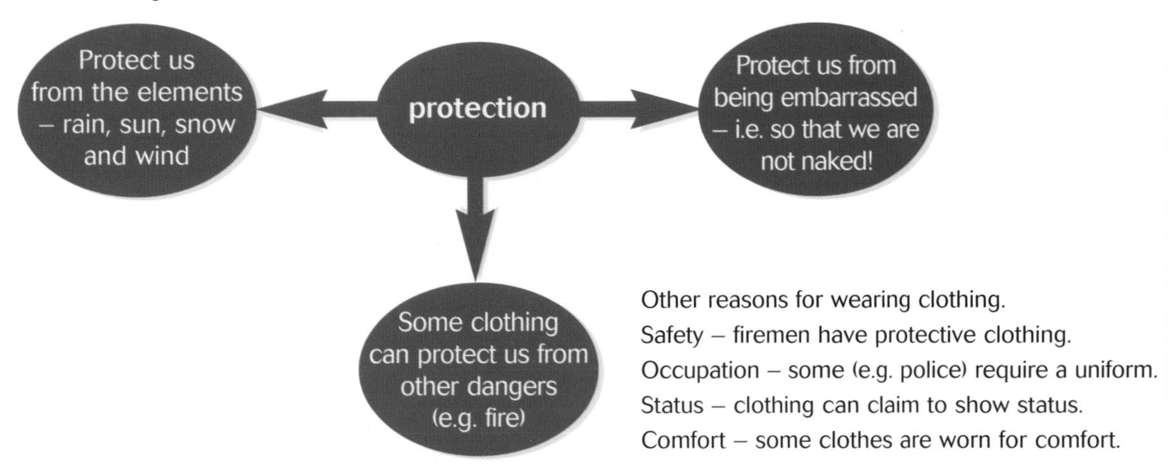

Other reasons for wearing clothing.
Safety – firemen have protective clothing.
Occupation – some (e.g. police) require a uniform.
Status – clothing can claim to show status.
Comfort – some clothes are worn for comfort.

The following groups and individuals have particular needs for clothing and footwear:

Babies

Babies find it difficult to control and maintain their body temperatures. For this reason they should be dressed in several layers of thin clothing which can be added to or removed in order to help maintain body temperature. For example, in warmer weather the number of layers should be reduced to prevent overheating.

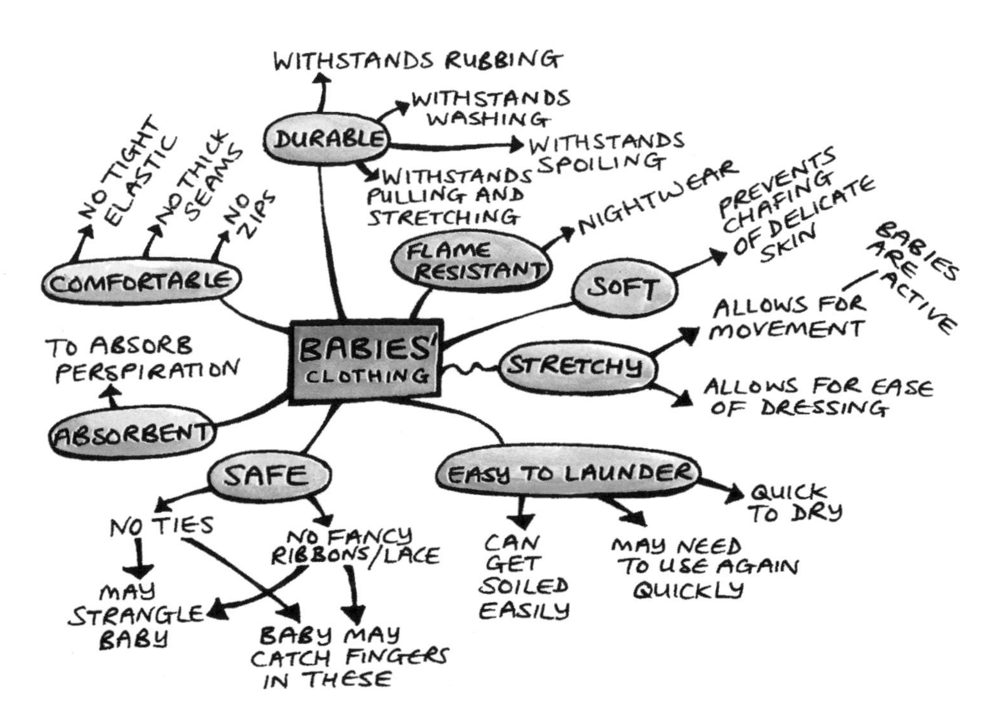

Design features to consider:

- Are fastenings easy to use (e.g. poppers and velcro)?
- Baby-grows are good as they meet most of the requirements shown in the above mind map.
- Trousers can be padded at the knees to prevent chafing when crawling.
- Babies do not need shoes until they start walking. Shoes must fit well so that they support the baby's feet and do not cause deformation of the feet. Ideally have the baby's feet measured regularly.
- Baby-grows and socks must fit well.

Toddlers/Young Children

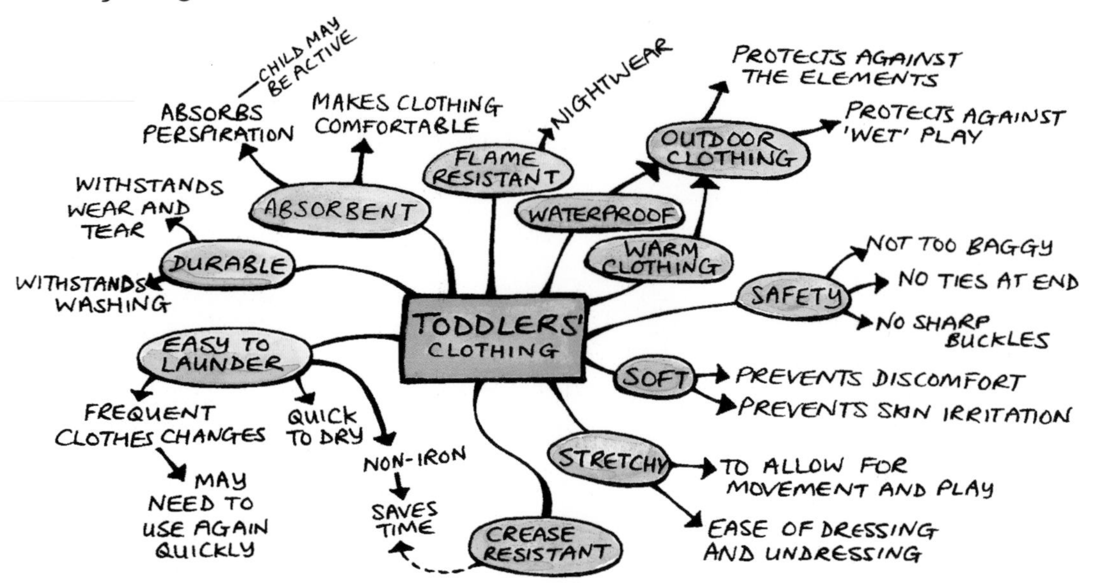

Design features to consider:

- May still be wearing nappies, so access for changing is important – dungarees or trousers with leg poppers.
- Elasticated waist bands – allow for ease of dressing/undressing.
- Fastenings – easy to use (e.g. velcro and large buttons encourage independence when dressing).
- Clothing should allow for stretching and movement when playing (e.g. jogger bottoms).
- Jackets should not have neck ties, etc. which may cause an accident.
- Nightwear should allow freedom of movement/comfort.
- Footwear and socks should be well fitting. A shoe shop can provide specialist advice.
- Velcro fastenings on footwear encourage independence.

Adolescents/Teenagers

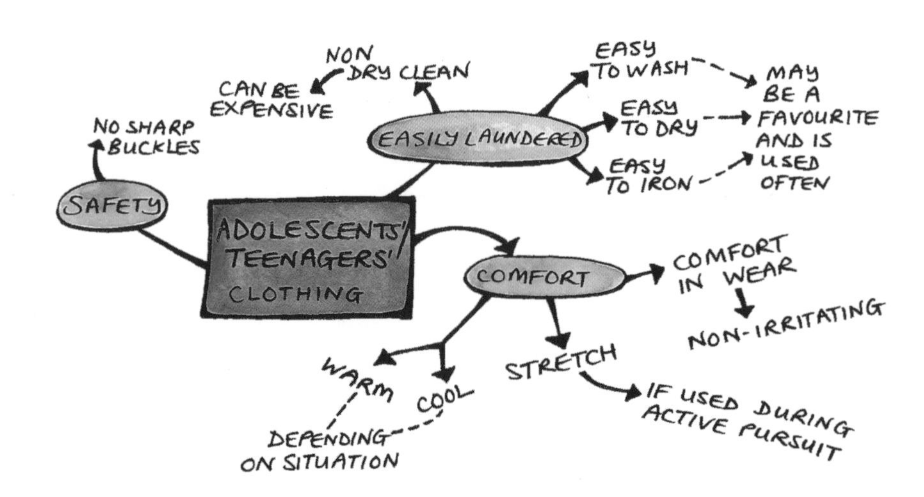

Design features to consider:

- The above mind map for teenagers' and adolescents' clothing is much smaller than those of other groups. This is because what teenagers will buy will be dependent on many different factors that we have already discussed. These include cost, colour, peer pressure and family pressure.
- Teenagers are often involved in a variety of differing activities so clothing may need to be multi-functional.
- One of the trends of the past ten years has been an increase in the purchase of designer clothing by teenagers.
- Some clothing may be considered for purchase that defies normal conventions (e.g. oversized/baggy clothing).
- Fashions tend to be cyclical – some fashions come and go, so clothing bought will work or not depending on the fashion cycle of the time.
- Footwear should fit well – even allowing for fashion!

Adults

Clothing for adults will vary from individual to individual. There are no particular design features that are particular to adults. The properties required from clothing will be determined by the factors that we have already discussed such as income, size and lifestyle.

Elderly People

The elderly person may not have any particular requirements for clothing. Many elderly people lead very active and full lives. Others may have problems with mobility; some may have particular illnesses, such as arthritis, and these will pose particular requirements for elderly people when considering clothing.

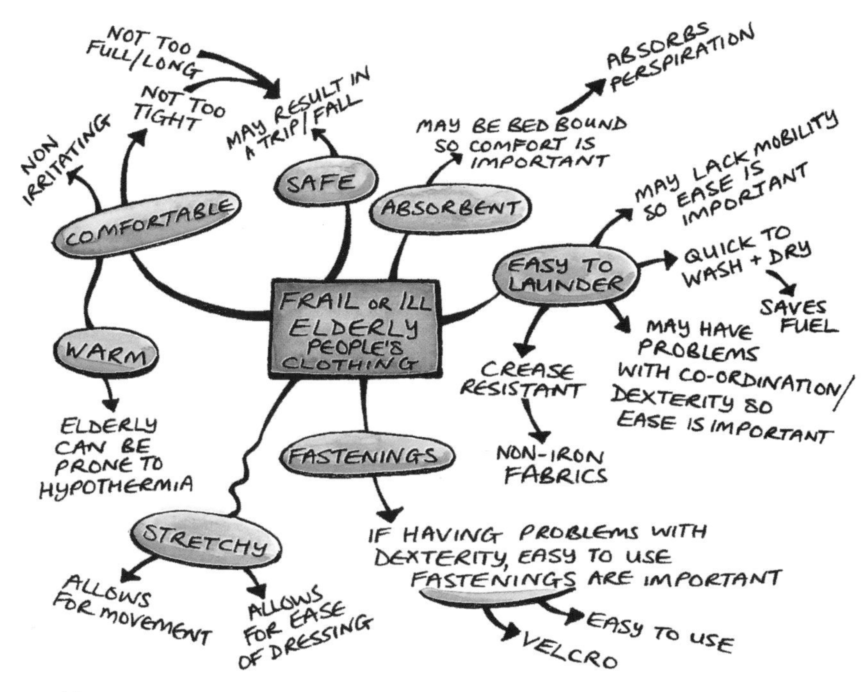

Design features to consider:

- These will vary from individual to individual.
- Elasticated waistband may be important to ease dressing if mobility/dexterity is a problem.
- Front-fastening garments may be easier to use than back-fastening garments.
- Outdoor clothing should be warm and prevent draughts (e.g. elasticated cuffs and waistband).
- People who lack mobility may have problems keeping warm. They should be encouraged to wear several thin layers of clothing, wear thermal underwear and if necessary a hat and gloves.
- Shoes should fit properly – flat shoes are ideal.
- Shoes should be maintained to ensure they have good grips to prevent slipping.
- Slip-on shoes may be advantageous because they are easy to put on with little physical effort needed from bending down or tying laces if individuals are suffering from arthritis or other conditions.

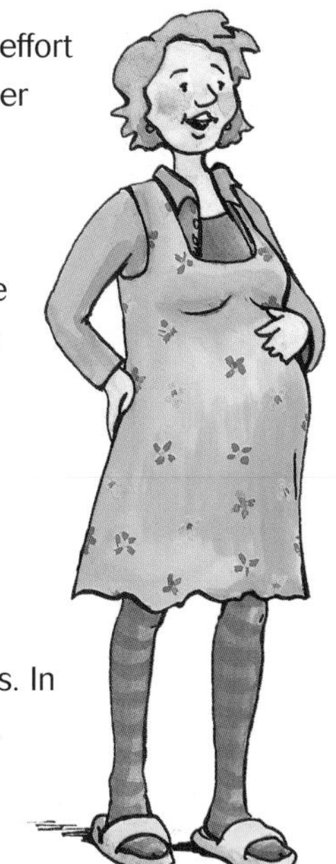

Pregnant and Breastfeeding Women

During pregnancy, women become larger and heavier. Mobility may also be reduced in the later stages of pregnancy. There are a number of factors that need to be considered when selecting clothing for pregnant women:

- Clothing should be loose fitting to allow for comfort and movement.
- Elasticated bands allow additional comfort and support.
- Fastenings should be able to be adjusted to provide comfort.
- Fabric should be soft and stretchy to accommodate the increased body size and provide comfort.
- Clothing should be easy to launder as this will prevent having to purchase many clothes. In the later stages of pregnancy, having clothing that is easy to launder may be important.
- Shoes should provide support and fit well as there is extra weight to be carried.
- Flat shoes are ideal.
- When breastfeeding, garments which allow easy access to the breasts are important.

Individuals with Physical Disabilities

The individual needs of those with physical disabilities will vary depending on the type of disability. The needs of a person with a broken arm vary considerably from those of a person with limited sight. When answering this type of question, think about the following factors:

- What is the physical disability?
- How will this affect the clothing to be purchased?
- Are there problems with dressing? (In this case stretch and fastening are important.)
- Is the person mobile? (You need to think about safety, absorbency and ease of laundering.)
- Will the garment be subject to particular stresses, for example rubbing? (In this case durability is an important consideration.)

You will need to think about the problem carefully and plan your answer before writing. Remember that the question paper contains space for rough work. Use this space to plan your work.

When thinking about the properties of textiles for clothing and footwear, there are a number of different factors that need to be considered:

- protection
- comfort
- suitability for purpose
- safety.

Protection

We use textiles to protect us from the environment. Textiles keep us cool, warm and dry. When we wear clothing we tend to adjust what we wear to suit different climatic conditions and so suit the environment in which we will be wearing the clothes, i.e. indoor or outdoor.

Keeping warm/keeping cool/keeping dry

In order to keep the body warm, clothing must be able to insulate the body. This can be achieved by trapping a layer of air inside the clothing. When we wear clothes and take part in activities, we perspire. Clothing has an important role to play in the removal of this perspiration. Some fabrics can absorb this moisture and then release the moisture to the outside where it evaporates.

- Layering – when faced with cold climatic conditions, wearing a number of thin layers of clothing can help maintain warmth. Each layer of clothing will trap air and so insulate the body.
- Fibres – some fibres can trap air and so are naturally warm (e.g. wool). Other fibres naturally absorb moisture and so help to keep the body dry (e.g. cotton).
- Fabric construction – this can affect the amount of air trapped. Knitted products, for example, trap larger amounts of air and so tend to insulate the body well.
- Fabric finishing – some fabrics can be treated to help them retain warmth or repel water.

Specific examples:

Quilting

This is often used on duvets and anoraks. One way of ensuring good insulation is to use quilted fabric. Wadding is sewn between two layers of fabric. This wadding traps a large amount of air and so provides a good insulating layer.

Fleece fabrics

Used in sweatshirts, dressing gowns and outdoor jackets. These are lightweight fabrics, which have a fleecy soft backing which is comfortable to the skin. Air is trapped in this fleece backing and so keeps the body warm.

Microfibres

These are very fine synthetic fibres. They can be used alone or mixed with other fibres. These microfibres are ideal for the manufacture of waterproof products. The fibres are woven tightly creating small air traps, which prevent rain and wind getting in but at the same time allow water vapour from the body to escape. This results in both warmth and dryness in clothing which makes the process suitable for all types of outdoor clothing (e.g. hillwalking jackets, ski wear).

Microporous membranes

These are membranes which can be applied or added to a wide range of fabrics. The advantage of these membranes is that they prevent water and wind getting into the clothing, but allow perspiration to travel to the outside of the clothing where it can evaporate. This helps to keep the body dry and warm.

There are specific design features that can be added to garments to assist in keeping you warm, cool or dry.

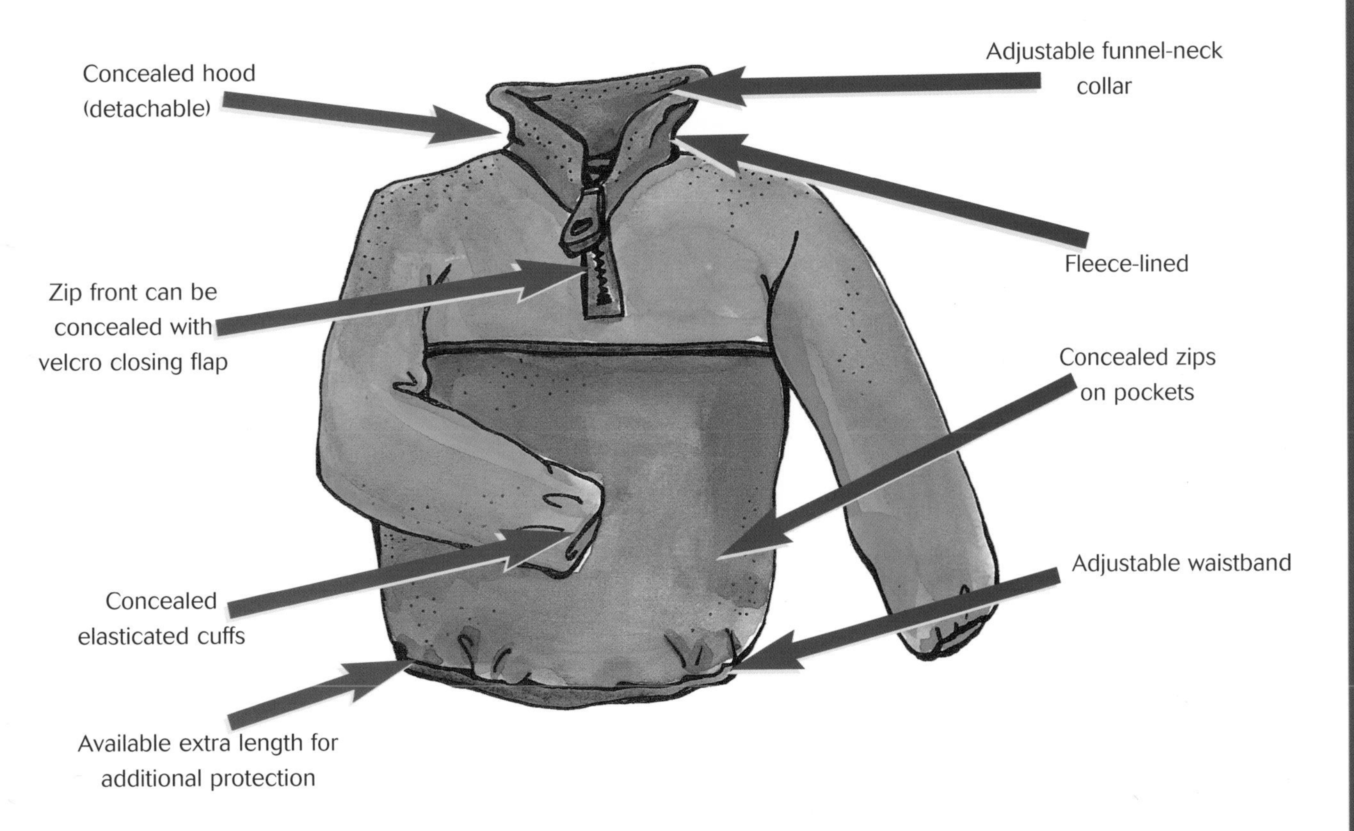

Comfort and Fit

As well as thinking about protection, we need to consider comfort and fit when selecting clothes. There are a number of factors that affect comfort.

Softness	How the fabric feels to the touch. Some fabrics, such as silk, feel very soft and smooth when next to the skin, whilst others might tickle or scratch. Some of the new fleece fabrics are designed to give a very soft feel next to the skin.
Absorbency	Fibres that can absorb moisture (perspiration) from the skin, and then carry this moisture to the outside of the clothing to evaporate, will aid comfort. Some synthetic fibres have poor absorbency and can lead to a feeling of clamminess or wetness.
Weight	The weight of the fabric can assist with comfort. Some of the newer fleece sports tops are designed to be very lightweight while still keeping you warm and dry. This is important for activities such as hillwalking where added weight could lead to discomfort.
Elasticity	Elasticity is an important property for some garments. Where the body needs a good degree of freedom to move and stretch, it is important that the clothing we wear allows this freedom of movement. Aerobics outfits, for example, need to have this property. Not only do they allow stretching, but they also retain their shapes. Garments which have elastane added to them also tend to hug the body. This can be advantageous in a swimming costume which needs to be drag resistant so helping to improve performance.
Size	The size of the garment is important. When a garment is too tight in certain areas (e.g. the waist), it can lead to a feeling of discomfort. We are not all the same size and so clothes tend to come in a variety of sizes. Specialist shops are available for people who are above or below the normal range of sizes. Some garments, such as jeans, are now produced using fibres including a small amount of elastomeric fibres. This provides a degree of stretch which can aid comfort.
Fastenings	There are many different types of fastening available. Manufacturers are usually careful in selecting fastenings which are appropriate to the garment and which aid comfort. Fastenings or labels which are inappropriately placed can lead to discomfort and irritation of the skin. It is always advisable to try clothing on before buying to ensure a good fit, but also to determine comfort. Fastenings should be easy to use. The type of fastening used is determined by the item. Zips, for example, would not be appropriate for a baby-grow as they are less flexible than poppers.
Crease Resistance	Psychological discomfort occurs when we feel that we are inappropriately dressed. Having clothing that is crease-free can be important in terms of feeling comfortable in the clothing that you are wearing. If you are packing clothing for a holiday, crease-resistant clothing will prevent you from having to pack a travel iron. Likewise, crease-resistant clothing is suitable if you are involved in an occupation where you are sitting for a long period of time.

Footwear considerations

Footwear should fit well. If it is to be comfortable, it is always advisable to get your feet measured before you buy new shoes. Many shoes come in different sizes and width fittings to ensure your comfort. Think about the following:

- Shoes which are made of natural materials allow feet to breathe.
- The grip on the shoes should be good to prevent slipping. This becomes more important if the shoes are to be used for specific activities such as hillwalking.
- Shoes should support and protect your feet. Your feet carry the weight of your whole body.
- Some footwear has adjustable fastenings, which can aid comfort.
- Outdoor shoes should be waterproof.
- Some trainers are made from breathable fabrics, which allow the feet to breathe and stay fresh and comfortable.
- Some trainers now incorporate visible air sole units, which protect the feet when playing sports.

Sometimes we select clothes for a particular occasion:

- for work
- for leisure
- for special occasions (e.g. a wedding).

It is important to think about the following factors:

- What will the item be used for?
- Will it require any special properties (e.g. flame/crease-resistance)?
- Are there any special design features it will need (e.g. pockets to carry objects)?
- Are there any other factors that you need to think about (e.g. colour, cost)?

Safety

Safety is always an important consideration when buying textile items. Here are some safety factors that you should think about.

Fabrics can be treated to make them flameproof. The fabric is treated with a chemical which will prevent the item catching fire if it is placed near a naked flame. Many fabrics used for soft furnishings (such as sofa beds and cushions) and nightwear are treated to stop them burning. The British Standards Institution lays down strict guidelines on the way fabrics should be produced for both nightwear and soft furnishings. These items will display a low flammability label or other appropriate warnings. Here are two examples:

LOW FLAMMABILITY TO
BS 5722

FLAME RESISTANT FINISH

As found on a child's night dress

KEEP AWAY
FROM FIRE

As found on a boy's pyjamas

Dressing gowns and night dresses tend to be loose fitting and so are at risk of catching fire from a naked flame (e.g. a living room fire).

This is an example of a label found attached to a sofa bed. These safety labels must be permanently attached to the product in addition to removable swing labels.

This product has been tested and meets the tests undertaken for flammability resistance.

This symbol means that the covers and fillings are cigarette- and match-resistant.

There are other factors that affect the safety of textile items:

- Fabrics which trap air tend to be more flammable. Therefore, items that are knitted or have a brushed surface tend to be more flammable.
- Wools and silks are generally flame-resistant, whereas cotton, linen and viscose are all flammable.
- Luminous or reflective strips can be added to clothing and accessories to ensure visibility.
- Bright colours are often used on hillwalking and mountaineering clothing to ensure visibility.
- Some fabrics can be coated (e.g. PVC coated aprons are often used in kitchens to protect against splashes).

Shelter

It is important that individuals and families have shelter, in whatever form this takes. We require shelter to protect us from the weather and to provide safe and secure places to live as family groups. Most forms of shelter provide us with the basic essentials that we need to ensure survival:

- warmth – generated from gas, electricity or oil
- water – provided directly to most forms of shelter
- provision of toilet facilities.

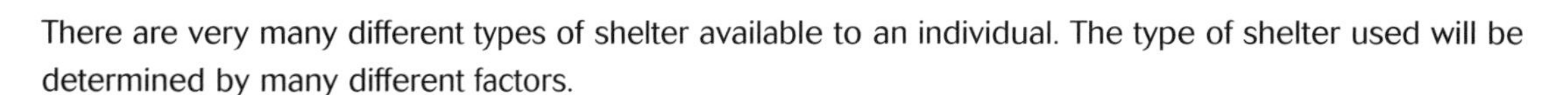

There are very many different types of shelter available to an individual. The type of shelter used will be determined by many different factors.

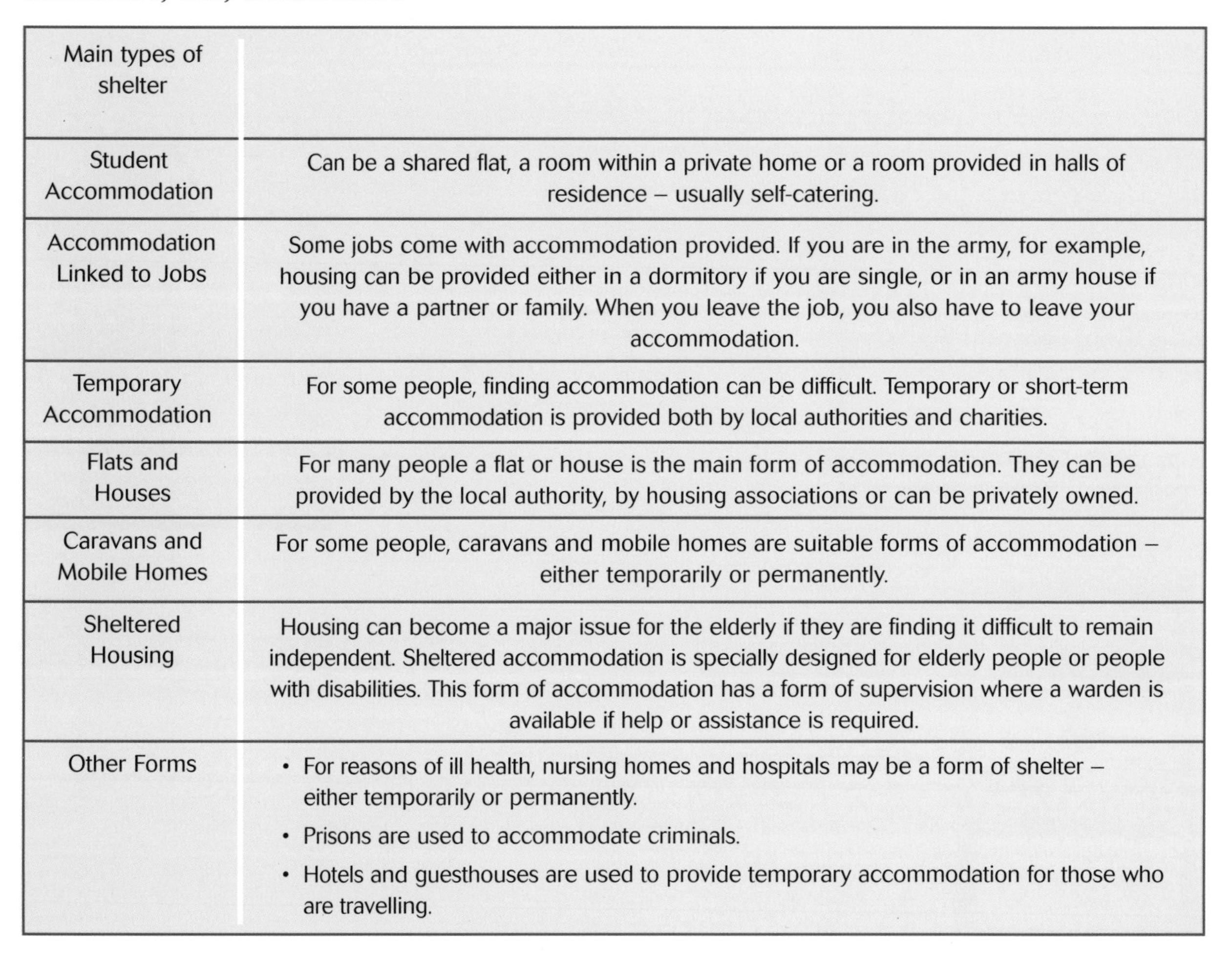

Main types of shelter	
Student Accommodation	Can be a shared flat, a room within a private home or a room provided in halls of residence – usually self-catering.
Accommodation Linked to Jobs	Some jobs come with accommodation provided. If you are in the army, for example, housing can be provided either in a dormitory if you are single, or in an army house if you have a partner or family. When you leave the job, you also have to leave your accommodation.
Temporary Accommodation	For some people, finding accommodation can be difficult. Temporary or short-term accommodation is provided both by local authorities and charities.
Flats and Houses	For many people a flat or house is the main form of accommodation. They can be provided by the local authority, by housing associations or can be privately owned.
Caravans and Mobile Homes	For some people, caravans and mobile homes are suitable forms of accommodation – either temporarily or permanently.
Sheltered Housing	Housing can become a major issue for the elderly if they are finding it difficult to remain independent. Sheltered accommodation is specially designed for elderly people or people with disabilities. This form of accommodation has a form of supervision where a warden is available if help or assistance is required.
Other Forms	• For reasons of ill health, nursing homes and hospitals may be a form of shelter – either temporarily or permanently. • Prisons are used to accommodate criminals. • Hotels and guesthouses are used to provide temporary accommodation for those who are travelling.

Reliable sources of consumer advice

When shopping for goods and services, there are times when you think it would be good to know a little more about your rights and responsibilities as a consumer. There are times when you might think that it would be good to have someone to talk to who can provide you with help and advice on consumer matters. There is lots of help and advice about and interesting information available on consumer issues.

The following bodies offer consumer advice. This advice is generally very reliable and up to date. These agencies all offer different types of advice and support.

Citizen's Advice Bureau (CAB)

The Citizen's Advice Bureau service offers free, independent and confidential advice. The CAB helps solve problems which are central to people's lives, including debt and consumer issues, benefits, housing, legal matters, employment, and immigration. Advisers can help fill out forms, write letters, negotiate with creditors and represent clients at court or tribunal. Ninety per cent of the advisers are volunteers. They include CAB advisers, administrators and management committee members.

Each CAB belongs to the National Association of Citizen's Advice Bureaux (NACAB), which sets standards for advice, training, equal opportunities and accessibility. The NACAB also produces a variety of free publications.

As well as giving advice, the NACAB uses its bank of client evidence to find out where local and national services and policies should change.

Each CAB is an independent charity, relying on funding from the local authority and from local businesses, charitable trusts and individual donations.

CABs are found in most main towns and cities. Most CABs now provide an online service. Many CABs operate on an appointment basis.

Consumer Advice Centre (CAC)

These can be organised by the local authority or be independent. They offer free and independent confidential advice to the consumer. Like CABs, CACs offer practical help on how you can deal with a wide range of consumer problems and issues as well as introducing you to other sources of help (e.g. organisations who can advise and assist you with specific problems). CACs can assist you with taking action and provide advice on using the Small Claims Court.

The staff at CACs are given specific training on issues relating to consumerism.

There are a number of Independent Consumer Advice Centres available and they rely on their funding from local authorities, local businesses and grants.

You can now get online help and advice from a variety of web sites.

Consumers' Association (CA)

The Consumers' Association (CA) was established in 1957 to provide pre-shopping help and assistance to consumers.

The CA carries out research and undertakes comprehensive testing of consumer products, ranging from cars to washing machines. These tests are independent and the results are published in a magazine called *Which?* The CA will independently test a range of similar products (e.g. dishwashers), and report the findings to the consumer. The report will provide a wide range of information including:

- prices
- design features
- test results for each product
- what they regard as the best buy.

Which? magazine also provides a wide range of consumer information, ranging from issues such as the genetic modification of food to the services provided by dentists.

The CA is a strong campaigner for the rights of the consumer. It undertakes research and acts as a pressure group to benefit the consumer.

The CA does not handle individual complaints unless you subscribe. To obtain *Which?* magazine you have to pay a monthly subscription. You can also subscribe to an online service called 'Online Which?'

Local libraries usually have copies of *Which?* magazine.

Consumer Protection Department/Trading Standards Department/ Environmental Health Department

Local authorities run these departments. The names given to these departments vary within each local authority. Originally these departments were split but in many areas their functions have been combined.

Consumer Protection Department/ Trading Standards Department

Trading Standards officers enforce a range of laws intended to promote fair trading, consumer protection and environmental safety.

The trading standards service aims to ensure that:

- Members of the public are not misled by false statements about goods (including food) or about services.
- Consumer goods, particularly electrical appliances, toys and furniture, are constructed to high safety specifications.
- Honest traders are not put at a disadvantage by having to compete with misdescribed, counterfeit or dangerously shoddy goods.
- The storage and sale of dangerous products such as petroleum, explosives and poisons do not put the public or environment at risk.
- Overloaded lorries do not cause danger to the public or damage to roads and bridges.
- Certain animal diseases such as foot and mouth, bovine spongiform encephalopathy (BSE), and in particular rabies, do not enter or spread through the country.

The department provides a free and confidential advice and assistance service to anyone needing help to resolve disputes with traders, suppliers or other commercial organisations on trading standards related matters. They can also provide advice with debt problems.

Environmental Health Department

The Environmental Health Department (EHD) is responsible for protecting and improving the environment by providing environmental public health services.

Environmental Health Officers (EHOs) carry out statutory enforcement and advisory work. The services provided in this area concern:

- food safety
- occupational health & safety
- public health
- pollution
- dog control
- animal health.

EHOs work through inspection and enforcement – checking food standards and hygiene to prevent food poisoning, ensuring housing standards, monitoring pollution, enforcing Occupational Health and Safety regulations and running the Dog Warden and Pest Control Services.

EHOs are also involved in education rather than just enforcing the rules and they work closely with schools, community organisations and other bodies on local environment and public health issues.

National and Scottish Consumer Council

The Council is a non-departmental public body, set up by the UK government in 1975. A large part of the Council's funding is grant-in-aid from the Department of Trade and Industry. It aims to:

- promote action for furthering and safeguarding the interests of consumers;
- ensure that those who take decisions which will affect consumers have balanced and authoritative views of the interests of consumers before them;
- insist that the interests of all consumers, including the inarticulate and disadvantaged, are taken into account.

It does not deal with individual complaints but does look at issues that concern consumers. The NCC acts as a pressure group. The NCC has a separate Scottish office.

Consumer rights and responsibilities

Sale and Supply of Goods Act 1994

This law provides the consumer with three areas of protection when buying goods and services. The goods must be:

- of satisfactory quality
- fit for the intended purpose
- as described.

When you buy goods from a shop, market stall, garage etc, the law says they have to be of satisfactory quality. The satisfactory quality test includes the appearance and finish of the goods, their safety and durability. Goods must be free from defects, even minor ones, unless the seller has pointed them out to you, and fit for all their intended purposes – including any purpose the seller told you about.

The law also gives you a **reasonable** time to reject goods if they're faulty. What is '**reasonable**' is not a fixed period of time but will depend on their cost and complexity. Normally you can take your purchase home and make sure it is satisfactory but, if you delay examining it or telling the seller about a fault, you may lose your right to reject it and a refund of your money.

Incidentally, letting the seller have a go at putting faulty goods right has no effect on your legal right to reject them. If you take the goods back promptly and the seller's attempt to repair them fails, you can still reject the goods – but you must act promptly.

Your rights when buying used goods or from a sale are exactly the same as if you bought them new. Naturally, the law takes the view that you can't expect them to be as durable or have the same appearance and finish as new goods, but they should still work properly in relation to their age and previous usage.

Trade Descriptions Act 1968 and 1972

It is an offence to apply a false trade description to goods or to supply goods to which a false trade description is applied. It is an offence if an employer or trader or employee falsely describes the goods he or she is selling, for example selling a product as organic when in fact it is not. The Act also makes it illegal for traders to knowingly mislead you about the services that they provide (e.g. advertising free delivery but then actually charging for delivery).

Consumer Protection Act 1987

This Act ensures consumers have rights to compensation for death or injury caused by using defective consumer goods. This Act applies not only to the person or organisation from whom the goods were purchased but also includes the manufacturer or importer. The Act establishes a 'general safety requirement', namely that all goods for domestic use must be reasonably safe, bearing in mind all the circumstances.

Powers under the Act allow suspect goods to be 'suspended' from sale for up to six months, while checks on safety are conducted. If faulty, the goods may be destroyed.

These safety provisions have been extended to cover all consumer goods and require all domestic consumer goods to be safe.

The Act regulates price indications for goods, services, accommodation or facilities. Businesses must not give consumers misleading price indications.

Food Safety Act 1990

The Food Safety Act protects consumers in that it states that food must not:

- injure the health of consumers
- be unfit for human consumption – i.e. it ensures that all food produced and sold is safe to eat
- be contaminated in any form.

The Food Safety Act increases the powers available to enforcement agencies and increases legal powers.

The Act ensures that the employer and the employee:

- do not do anything to the food to make it harmful
- do not sell food that is not as is stated (e.g. selling 'steak mince' that is actually beef mince);
- do not describe food in a way that will mislead consumers.

The Act covers all food premises from shops to restaurants and applies to anyone working in a food business, whether it be a small sandwich-making stall or a large food manufacturing company.

Food Safety (General Food Hygiene) Regulations 1995

These regulations are designed to ensure that all food businesses operate in a safe and hygienic manner. The regulations state that food businesses have to assess all the potential risks that there might be in making their products. These are risks that would contaminate the food product in any way. Once these risks are identified, the business has to take appropriate action to prevent contamination.

Food Safety (Temperature Control) Regulations 1995

These state that chilled foods must be kept at a temperature no greater than 8°C in order to prevent micro-organism development. It also states that cooked or reheated food which is to be sold must be kept above 63°C at all times.

Food Hygiene (General) Regulations 1995

These regulations ensure that the equipment and premises that are involved in the production of food are kept very clean. The Regulations lay down specific standards that must be followed in the design and equipping of a food business. The regulations deal with the following areas:

- premises
- equipment
- food handlers
- washing facilities
- services
- practices.

Labelling of products

This section deals with the labelling of consumer products. It details what the law requires and what is additional.

Food Products

By law, a food product must show the following information:

An ingredients list, with the list in descending order of weight (i.e. the first ingredient is the largest by weight)

Product name or description of what the product is

Storage
structions

Origin of product

Instructions for use (if required)

Name and address of manufacturer, packer or EC seller

Product Weight

Indication of the shelf life (i.e. Best Before or Use By date)

Additional information on food labelling

- The 'e' beside the weight means that the average quantity must be accurate but the weight of each pack may vary slightly.
- In the ingredients list, any additives that have been used in the product must be listed, stating what their job is (e.g. preservative = potassium sorbate).
- Flavourings do not have numbers so they must be stated.
- Nutritional information is optional but most companies provide it. If it is provided, it must meet certain criteria.
- If a product makes a specific claim (e.g. 'extra fruit') the label must show the minimum amount of fruit in the product.

Other symbols found on food products

This symbol is used to show that foods have been produced organically (i.e. aims to avoid the use of artificial or synthetic chemicals).

Bar codes are now used on most products. They are used to check the level of stock in a supermarket. When a product is sold, the bar code is scanned. This tells the supermarket that this product has been sold and allows the store to order new stock.

This symbol reminds us that we should be disposing of our litter in a way that helps to protect the environment.

This symbol means that the product is suitable for vegetarians, but not necessarily for vegans.

This symbol means that the product has been approved by the Vegan Society as being suitable for vegans.

The microwave labelling system

As from 1992, all domestic microwave ovens have had to carry a new label, similar to the one detailed below. All food products which carry microwave-cooking instructions make reference to this labelling scheme.

The label tells us the following information:

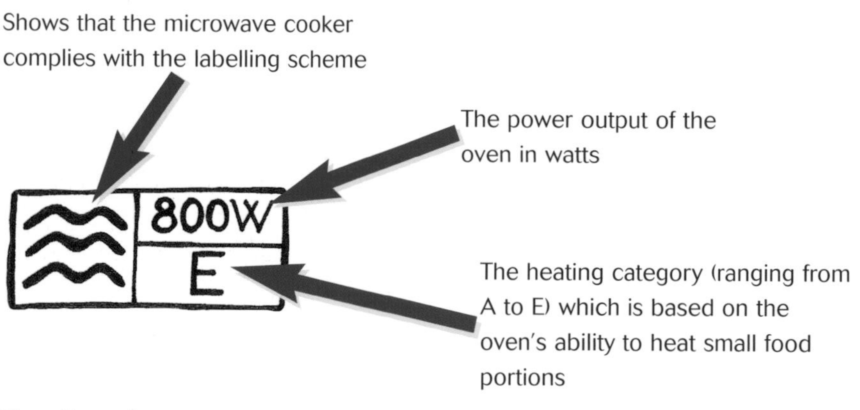

An 800W oven will cook faster than a 500W oven.

If your oven is rated D it will heat up small portions of food faster than one rated B.

How it works

Packaged food that can be cooked in the microwave will be marked with the microwave symbol. The pack will also give instructions for heating using both the power rating and the heating category.

TO MICROWAVE	HEAT ON FULL POWER	STAND
800W E	4-5 MINUTES	1 MINUTE
650W C	5-6 MINUTES	1 MINUTE

For this product, you would cook the food for 4–5 minutes if your microwave cooker was an 800W cooker or had a heat category of E.

If your microwave cooker had a heat category D, then you would cook the food for approximately 5 minutes.

You must remember that food must always be piping hot.

Other labels

The following labels can be seen on a variety of products:

The Lion Mark

As part of the drive towards consumer awareness the British Toy and Hobby Association introduced the Lion Mark in 1989, establishing a symbol of safety and quality designed to warn the British consumer against the pitfalls of buying faulty toys for their children. A toy carrying the Lion Mark on itself or its packaging is made by a reputable manufacturer who adheres to a strict code of practice. This ensures that the manufacturer's toys are made to the highest standards of safety in force in the UK and Europe (currently BS EN 71). Toys bought from an Approved Lion Mark Retailer indicate that all toys in that shop conform to the Lion Mark standard.

The Toy Safety Regulations 1995 state that all toys manufactured and supplied within the EU must be tested to ensure they meet minimum standards of safety. Only products that meet these criteria can bear the CE mark and so be sold in the EU. Where the toy is small, or contains small parts, this must be clearly indicated on the toy or on the toy packaging.

The CE mark is also displayed on a wide variety of other products. This marking is found on electrical appliances which meet the minimum safety standards. The CE mark is an indication that the product has been manufactured to meet the minimum requirements of safety regulations. The CE mark does not guarantee the quality of the product, nor should it be seen as a suitable replacement for other safety marks.

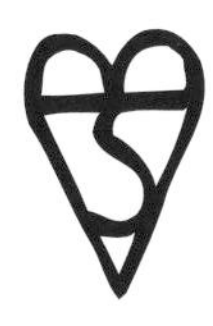

This is the Kitemark of the British Standards Institution. Firms can apply to have this mark added to their products. This means that the product has been rigorously checked and tested to ensure that the product is manufactured to required standards in terms of safety, quality and reliability. Continual checks are made on products that display the Kitemark.

The British Electrotechnical Approvals Board (BEAB)

BEAB is the UK's leading body in the safety approvals industry for electrical products used in the home. The BEAB Approved Mark assures consumers that products have undergone rigorous independent testing, annual factory inspection and on-going surveillance which meet both European and international safety standards.

Manufacturers of domestic electrical appliances can apply for BEAB Approval on a wide range of products including domestic appliances, consumer electronics, IT equipment and lighting.

Products such as hair dryers do not always contain an earth wire. If this is so, the product should carry this double insulation symbol. This means that the product has been manufactured in such a way to ensure that the risk of shock from using the product is minimised.

Dangerous products, such as bleach and other household cleaners, have to carry warning labels indicating that they can be dangerous if not used correctly according to the instructions given. These symbols mean that the product is harmful if swallowed and can cause irritation to the skin.

This symbol means that the product is toxic and can cause serious harm if swallowed.

The Eco-Label

This label is found on products such as dishwashers and washing machines to show that they have been designed and manufactured with the environment in mind. These products will have features added to use less energy, less water and less detergent, and so are better for the environment.

The British Gas Corporation Seal of Service

Every gas appliance sold by an authorised or registered dealer will display this label. It ensures the safety of the appliance, the installation of the appliance and the provision of spare parts when needed.

The Council for Registered Gas Installers (CORGI)

CORGI is the body given the responsibility by the Health and Safety authorities to maintain a register of competent gas installers in Great Britain, Northern Ireland and the Isle of Man. It is a legal requirement for businesses carrying out gas work to be registered with CORGI.

CORGI introduced a mandatory ID card in 1999 which allows the consumer to check the operative is registered before entering the property. From April 2002 the ID card will also contain information in braille to help visually impaired consumers.

General wellbeing

There are a number of factors which combine together to ensure that we have good health:

- sleep
- a well-balanced diet
- fresh air and exercise
- personal cleanliness
- general good habits.

Some of these factors have been discussed fully in other sections. In this section we will look at sleep, exercise and general good habits.

Sleep

Our bodies need to rest. Even when we are resting and sleeping, our bodies are still functioning – our basic bodily functions still have to work. When we sleep, our bodily activities slow down so that the body can go to work repairing and replacing damaged cells. The amount of sleep that we need varies from person to person. However the older we are, the less sleep we usually need. For example, babies sleep a great deal of the time whilst adults may get by on between six to eight hours per day. Other factors such as state of health, occupation and climate will also affect the amount of sleep that we require.

In order to get a good night's sleep there are some simple rules that should be followed:

- Try to wind down before going to bed. Working until late and then going straight to bed may result in a sleepless night.
- Try not to eat fatty or filling foods before going to bed. Your digestive system will have to work overtime to digest this food, and this can lead to poor sleep.
- A well-ventilated room will assist sleep.
- A warm bed also helps. If you are feeling tired and go into a cold bed, the end result might be that you feel wide-awake again!

Fresh air and exercise

Fresh air and exercise are good for the body. Not only do they help tone your muscles but they can help you to relax and sleep.

Fresh air is good for you as it ensures that the air you are breathing in is fresh and oxygen rich. This will help you to feel more alert.

Exercise in all forms, from running and swimming to dancing and playing golf, is good for the body:

- It gives you strength and vitality.
- It helps you to sleep.
- It can help you to reduce weight as you will burn up energy.
- It improves stamina.
- It tones the muscles and makes the heart, lungs and other muscles work more efficiently.
- It can aid your appetite.
- It can help you obtain good skin – through the action of sunlight on the skin.
- It can help to reduce stress.

Remember that if you are suffering from an illness it is important to seek medical attention before starting a vigorous exercise programme.

General good habits

By general good habits we mean looking after the body. There are many different substances that can cause harm to the body:

- alcohol
- drugs
- smoking.

Alcohol

Current advice suggests that light consumption of alcohol can in fact be good for the body. Some types of beer and wine contain chemicals that help in the fight against heart disease. When alcohol consumption is heavy it can lead to a variety of health-related problems. Excessive alcohol consumption can lead to dependency on it and this leads to addiction.

A person who experiences a strong desire to drink alcohol is known as an alcoholic – he or she suffers from alcoholism. Alcoholics can drink a lot of alcohol. If no alcohol is taken the sufferer experiences withdrawal symptoms which may include shaking, sweating and nausea. Excess alcohol can lead to health problems including:

- depression
- liver cirrhosis (hardening and enlargement of the liver)
- heart failure.

It may also lead to family and other relational breakdowns.

Pregnant women are advised not to drink in early pregnancy as this can have bad effects on the developing baby including possible deformity.

Smoking

Smoking kills over 120,000 people in the UK each year. Cigarettes contain more than 4000 chemical compounds and at least 400 toxic substances. While the smoker is inhaling, a cigarette burns at 700°C at the tip and around 60°C in the core. This heat breaks down the tobacco to produce various poisons.

The products of cigarettes that are most damaging to health are tar (which can cause lung cancer), carbon monoxide and nicotine (which can cause heart and circulatory diseases) other gases and tiny particles which cause smoker's lung. (This is where you cough a lot (sometimes daily) you easily get short of breath and your sputum is thick and difficult to cough up.)

Other health hazards related to smoking include:

- coronary thrombosis (a blood clot in the arteries which can lead to heart disease)
- atherosclerosis (clogging up of the arteries which can lead to a stroke)
- high blood pressure
- kidney failure
- cancer – not only of the lung but also of the oesophagus, the kidneys, the pancreas, the cervix and the bladder
- bad breath, stained teeth and a strong smell of cigarette smoke.

Research has shown that smoking reduces life expectancy by seven to eight years. The good news though is that by giving up smoking at any stage the rates of decline in lung capacity are reduced and this in turn postpones disability and handicap.

Drugs

At some time during our lives we take medicines to stop headaches, or we take pills and drugs prescribed by doctors. Whilst it is important not to rely on these products, they can bring some benefit to our lives.

Drug abuse is the use of a drug for purposes for which it was not intended, or using a drug in excessive quantities. All sorts of different drugs can be abused, including illegal drugs such as heroin or cannabis, prescription drugs such as tranquillisers or painkillers, and other medicines that can be bought from the supermarket such as cough mixtures or herbal remedies. Some medications – for example certain sleeping pills and painkillers – are addictive. They have an effect on the body which leads to addiction and withdrawal symptoms. Others may lead to a psychological addiction if people have a craving for the effect that the drug gives.

All drugs carry risks:

- The effects may be unexpected.
- Many drugs sold 'on the street' have been mixed with other substances, so users can never be sure what they're getting.
- Users may become tolerant to some drugs (e.g. heroin and speed). This means their bodies have become so used to the drug they need to take more to get the effect they want.
- Users may overdose (take too much for their bodies to handle). With heroin, gases, glues and aerosols an overdose can be fatal.

Drugs can lead to very many different health problems including: becoming overheated, dehydrated, drowsy, faint or unconscious and contracting HIV and hepatitis B or C. Injecting can also damage veins.

Management of expenditure

Budgeting

Sources of income

Household expenditure

Identifying priorities

Purchasing goods and services

Debt management →

Budgeting

Budgeting is about balancing the amount of money that comes into a house with that being spent. The ideal position to be in is to have a small amount of money left over each month that can be saved. Balancing the budget is what a household should be aiming for. If a household is constantly spending more money than is coming in, then the household will end up in debt.

Sources of income

We can classify income according to whether it is fixed – i.e. usually remains the same from month to month, or

variable – i.e. changes from month to month.

When planning a budget it is better to rely on income, which is guaranteed, i.e. fixed income.

If a person is employed, he or she will earn an income. Depending on the job, he or she will be paid a wage or a salary. People on wages tend to be paid a fixed rate for each hour worked. This will then be paid to the worker at the end of each week. This may be paid in cash but more likely it will be paid directly into a bank account. A person who is on a salary will be paid a fixed amount each year and this will usually be paid in 12 installments, i.e. every month. This is most likely to be paid directly into a bank account.

No matter how you get paid, you will get a wage slip. This details how much money you have earned. The wage slip will also show what deductions have been made. These deductions will be:

- Income Tax – everybody who earns above a certain amount of money has to pay income tax to the government.
- National Insurance – every person who earns above a certain amount of money has to pay national insurance to the government.
- Pension payments – some companies operate a pension scheme for employees. If you have agreed to enter one of these schemes (called superannuation schemes) money will be deducted from your earnings.

The money you get paid before your deductions is called your gross income.
The money you get paid after your deductions is called your net income.

Other sources of income:

Pensions – some people may be entitled to a state or private pension. When you retire you are entitled to a state pension. Money will be paid to you by the government. People who have set up a private pension fund will be paid an additional amount from this fund.

Interest – if you have a savings account or a current account that pays interest you will receive interest on a monthly basis. This amount of money will vary depending on what you are saving.

Dividends – some people buy shares in companies. They pay out dividends (similar to interest payments) on a regular basis. The amount paid out varies considerably.

Benefits – people who are on low incomes, who are unemployed or who are too ill to work, will be paid money by the government. This will vary depending on what benefit you are on and how much money you have saved.

Household expenditure

As well as classifying expenditure according to whether it is fixed or variable, we can also classify it according to whether it is

E essential – i.e. a type of expenditure that we must pay,

or

N non-essential – i.e. a type of expenditure that we could do without.

This table summarises the main areas of personal, family and household expenditure.

Expenditure Area	Fixed or Variable	Essential or Non-essential	Comments
Food	V	E	We need food to survive. Food can provide us with the correct balance of nutrients, depending on the choices we make. Food bills vary with the family size and the age and sex of the people in the house. Some food costs can be reduced through shopping around and wise buying but savings can be made from other areas first.
Clothing	V	E	We need clothing for warmth and protection from the elements. The amount of money spent on clothing will vary depending on the age and sex of the people in the household. Some savings can be made in this area but only after non-essential areas have been reduced.
Shelter	F	E	We need shelter to protect us and keep us safe and secure. This part of the budget normally includes rent or mortgage payments. This is an area where it is difficult to make any savings. If you do not make these payments you may not have a home to stay in.
Maintenance of Shelter	V	E	This includes the following categories of expenditure: • general maintenance costs • household cleaning • repairs. It is important that you make any repairs to your home that are necessary. This includes general maintenance and cleaning. If housing repairs are not undertaken, then the damage may get worse and indeed more expensive. Certain savings can be made in this area but not before all of the non-essential areas have been reduced.
Fuel	V	E	We need fuel to ensure that our houses remain warm and that we have fuel to cook with. The amount of fuel that we use will vary depending on the time of year. Most companies offer a monthly payment scheme whereby they estimate your fuel costs for the year and you pay this in installments. This can help with budgeting. You can now get your gas and electricity from the same supplier and they will usually give you a discount for this. You can make some savings in this area, but not before you have reduced spending in non-essential areas.
Taxes/ Insurance	F	E	• There are a number of taxes that you must pay. Income Tax and National Insurance are automatically deducted from your pay. You will also have to pay Council Tax. • If you have insurance policies it is advisable to keep up with these payments as in the longer term, they may make you some money.

Expenditure Area	Fixed or Variable	Essential or Non-essential	Comments
Transport	V	E or N	This section depends on your circumstances. If you rely on transport for getting to and from work then this area is essential. If, however, you could walk or cycle to work then this area may be less essential. Transport costs include the costs of motoring (e.g. road tax, MOT, car insurance, all of which you must have by law). Petrol costs and car maintenance will also be included here.
Debit and Credit Agreements	F	E	If you have any hire purchase agreements it is advisable to keep up with these payments, otherwise the goods may be taken from you. It is always advisable to make your credit payments on a regular basis. If you are experiencing problems, however, there are further steps that you can take. See page 107 for more information.
Personal Purchases	V	N	This category includes purchases that might be considered as non-essential or luxury items such as after-shave and perfume, cigarettes, alcohol, magazines. It would also include pets and pet food. These are items that we can normally do without if we need to save money.
Savings	V	N	It is good to have money to put aside for a 'rainy day'. It may not be possible to do so – particularly if you are finding it difficult to make ends meet.
Entertainment/ Sport/Leisure	V	N	This includes areas such as the cinema, theatre, bingo, going to pubs and nightclubs, as well as expenditure on sports such as football matches, golf, horse-riding, and so the list can go on. This category is where expenditure can be reduced.
Travel and Holidays	V	N	This is another category where expenditure can be reduced. Planning a holiday also means spending money and buying travel insurance and possibly new clothes.

Identifying priorities

It is important to remember that everybody has different sets of priorities. Those sections marked as essential are the main priorities that have to be considered when making a household budget. The areas marked as non-essential are the areas that can be easily reduced. We must also consider individuals' beliefs, values and preferences when developing a household budget. Here are two specific examples to explain this:

Household A is a very religious family. They set aside 10% of their net income for their church or temple. This would be reflected in the budget for this household.

Household B consists of an elderly man living alone. He has a pet dog. For this household, the dog will be an important consideration as it will provide companionship for the man, and will encourage him to go walking. This would be reflected in the budget for this household.

If, when the household budget is planned, there is an excess of income over expenditure, this excess can be budgeted as savings. If, however, there is an excess of expenditure over income, then savings will have to be made in the non-essential categories in order to get the budget to balance.

Purchasing goods and services

There are a wide variety of ways to pay for goods and services. The methods that people use will depend on the circumstances of the purchase and the needs of the individuals.

Main methods of payment

Method of Payment	Comments
Cash	• The easiest and most straightforward method of payment. You can only buy what you have available to spend. • If you are carrying large amounts of money, there is a possible danger of theft or loss of money.
Electronic Funds Transfer at Point of Sale (EFTPOS)	• Specific examples include SWITCH, DELTA and SOLO cards. • Anybody who has a suitable bank account can have an EFTPOS facility. This means you are given a debit card (a cash card) which allows you to pay for goods using the card. This plastic card stores your account details on a magnetic strip or microchip. When the card is swiped through the shop till, your bank account is instantly debited. With this method you can usually only spend up to the balance that is in your bank account.
Personal Cheque and Cheque Card	• Available to customers who hold a bank current account. You are normally provided with a cheque card, which acts as a guarantee to the shopkeeper that the cheque will be honoured by the bank (up to the limit indicated on the cheque card). • When paying for goods using this method, you write out a cheque detailing the amount of money to be paid in exchange for goods or services. • This money is then taken from your bank account a few days later. • This is a convenient method of paying for goods, but it is easy to write cheques and not have sufficient money in your bank account to cover the cheques you have written. This will normally result in a letter being sent to you from the bank.
Credit Card	• e.g. VISA and MASTERCARD • Usually only available to people who have a regular income and satisfy other requirements. • Each customer is given a credit limit. Purchases can be made up to this limit. • Each customer is given a plastic credit card, which holds your account details on a magnetic strip or microchip. The card is usually swiped through the till and the machine records your purchase details. Every month you are sent a statement showing the purchases you have made. This purchase balance can either be paid in full, or a portion of the sum can be paid. If you do not pay all the balance, you are charged interest on the balance remaining. • With this method of payment, it is **very** easy to get carried away and spend more than you can afford. • An annual fee may have to be paid.
Charge Card	• e.g. American Express • This works in a similar manner to a credit card. However the balance must be paid in full at the end of each month. • An annual fee may have to be paid.

Deferred payment systems

Method of Payment	Comments
Credit Sale	This is a common method of paying for goods on credit. It is only available from certain stores and only for those customers who meet certain criteria (i.e. those able to make repayments). A down payment is usually paid towards the cost of the items to be purchased. The balance is then paid over several months. Some companies offer interest free agreements. Like most forms of credit, it is very tempting to spend now and not be able to pay later. Fixed monthly payments assist with budgeting.
Hire Purchase (HP)	This is a common method of paying for goods on credit, particularly larger items such as cars. It is only available from certain stores and only for those customers who meet certain criteria. A down payment is usually paid towards the cost of the items to be purchased. The balance is then paid over several months. Interest is normally charged with HP agreements. Like most forms of credit it is very tempting to spend now and not be able to pay later. Fixed monthly payments assist with budgeting.
Store Budget Account	This is only available from certain stores and only to those customers who meet certain criteria. It works in the same way as a credit card, but you are limited as to where the card can be used. Consumers are given a credit limit for goods available for purchase from a particular store or groups of stores. Regular payments are made each month, and it is the amount of payment that is made that determines your credit limit. Interest is payable on outstanding balances. Interest charges can sometimes be quite high.
Store Charge Account	This works exactly like a credit card, but you can only use it in certain stores. Interest is payable on outstanding balances. Interest charges can sometimes be quite high.

By law, all companies offering credit have to display the rates of interest they charge. There is a set method of calculating this rate. This is called the Annual Percentage Rate of interest (APR). The APR allows customers to compare different rates of credit. The higher the APR, the more expensive the credit will be.

With a credit sale agreement you own the goods straight away. With HP you do not own the goods until the very last payment has been made. If you fall behind with your HP payments, the goods can be taken from you.

Many banks now offer customers smart cards. These are credit, debit and cash machine cards all in one. These allow you to access money from a cash machine 24 hours a day.

Credit, debit, and charge cards can be stolen and used by other people. Stolen cards should always be reported to the police.

You have to be over 18 to obtain credit.

Before offering you credit, companies will contact Credit Reference Agencies to check on your credit history. If you have had debt problems, you may find it difficult to obtain credit.

Advantages and disadvantages of buying goods by cash

Advantages	Disadvantages
• You can only buy what you can afford – you will not get into debt. • It is an easy and convenient way to pay for goods and services.	• Carrying large amounts of cash around can be dangerous. • Money can be accidentally lost. • It can be difficult to purchase items which are on special offer or reduced price if you are limited in the funds you have available.

Advantages and disadvantages of buying goods on credit

Advantages	Disadvantages
• It saves having to carry large amounts of cash around. • Used wisely, it can give you interest-free credit. • It can be used for emergencies or for picking-up sale bargains. • You may gain additional protection if you purchase items on credit (e.g. if you purchase an expensive item which proves to be faulty and the shop where you purchased it has closed down, you can make a claim from the credit provider). • You can use credit and charge cards to obtain cash from cash machines. (However, some banks will charge you for making a withdrawal.)	• You usually have to pay interest and so items cost more. • There are criteria that you have to meet before you can obtain credit. • It is easy to overspend and have problems repaying the debt. • Certain types of credit (e.g. credit and store cards) can be used fraudulently if lost or stolen. • Certain types of credit are not available for use in every store.

Whatever method of purchase you use, it always pays to shop around when buying goods and services, to ensure that you are getting the best value for money. Here are some simple tips:

Buying goods and services

- Look around different shops and stores to see the range available and to check prices.
- Use the Internet, mail order and TV shopping in order to compare prices of products.
- Use *Which?* magazine to get an idea of what is considered the 'best buy'.
- Ask friends or relatives for advice and information.
- Shop assistants can provide useful information, but this information may not always be reliable.

Shopping for groceries

- Buying in bulk from a cash and carry or supermarket may work out cheaper in the long term.
- Discount supermarkets stock less well known brands of foods, but they are usually less expensive.
- Make use of special offers if appropriate (e.g. buy two, get one free).
- Supermarket own brand products can often be cheaper than well-known brand-names.
- Money-off vouchers can help to reduce shopping bills. Even if you can't use them when shopping for food this week, keep them until you can.
- At the end of the shopping day, some products (e.g. bread) are sold at a reduced price.
- Some companies now offer free delivery and Internet food ordering.
- Local corner shops tend to be more expensive than supermarkets. However, they do sometimes have special offers and so shopping around can be useful.

Shopping for credit

- Investigate different lenders to get the best deal.
- Read the small print carefully.
- Think carefully about whether you will still be able to afford the repayments in a few months' time.
- Check the APR rates as well as other conditions (e.g. initial deposit to be paid and the period of repayment).

Debt management

When debt occurs, it can be a time of great worry and stress. If the debt is small, you may be able to adjust your household budget by reducing your expenditure on non-essential items. However, if the debt is getting out of control, you need to take a variety of steps.

1. Do not take on any further debt – this will only make your present situation worse.
2. Do not ignore letters and phone calls from your creditors (the people that you owe money to). The problem will not go away.
3. Contact all your creditors and let them know of your current financial difficulties. They may be able to assist you by extending the repayment period or reducing your monthly payments.
4. Keep records of all telephone calls made and copies of all correspondence.
5. Make a detailed note of your entire monthly income and expenditure. The credit companies may request that you send them this information before they can assist you. It will also let you have a clearer picture of what your financial situation is. It is important that your income and expenditure sheet is accurate and reliable.
6. If you are having real financial difficulties there is help and advice available.

Citizen's Advice Bureau (CAB)

CABs have specially trained advisers who can help you work your way through your debt problems. They can give you free advice and help. They will be able to help you draw up a debt management plan, based on your income and expenditure. The address and telephone number of the local CAB can be found in the telephone directory. See page 89 for more information on CABs.

Consumer Advice Centre (CAC)

These centres offer practical help and advice on a variety of shopping related matters. Staff are trained to offer free and confidential advice – including advice on debt management. See page 89 for more information on CACs.

Credit Union

Credit unions are set up in local communities to offer financial services to local people. They have trained staff who deal with money management issues and will be able to provide help and assistance. They may be able to refer you to another appropriate organisation for additional help and support.

Company/bank/building society concerned

We have already said that it is important to contact the people that you owe money to. When they are aware of your financial difficulties they will be able to work with you to help resolve your problems. Most credit lending bodies offer free advice and will be able to assist consumers in this situation.

Some companies advertise in the media, offering a service to assist consumers that have financial difficulties. They offer you a package of measures to reduce your monthly credit repayments. (They do not offer a loan, they simply deal with all your creditors and try to agree a reduced payment programme.) It is important to remember that these companies may charge you a monthly fee that you could be using to pay off your existing debt.

The Consumer Credit Counselling Service (CCCS) offers you a similar service, which is free. This service has the backing of most credit companies. You can find the telephone number of the CCCS in the telephone book.

Course content checklist

➜

Course content checklist

Use the following course content checklist when revising to ensure that you have covered all the essential knowledge that is required. Your exam papers will only test you on areas of the course content covered in the checklists.

Eating a variety of foods contributes to health

		✓
Main nutrients, their sources and functions	**11**	
Protein	11	
Carbohydrate: Sugar and Starch	11	
Fat	11	
Vitamin A: Retinol/Carotene	12	
Vitamin D	12	
Vitamin E	12	
Vitamin K	12	
Vitamin C	12	
Vitamin B group: B1/B2/Folic Acid	13	
Antioxidant vitamins	13	
Iron	13	
Calcium	14	
Fluoride	14	
Sodium	14	
Phosphorus	14	
Relationship between water, non-starch polysaccharides and health	**15**	
Water	15	
Non-starch polysaccharides	15	
Health and nutrient intake	**16**	
Health and Energy	16	
Health and Protein	16	
Multi-nutritional value of food	16	
Interrelationship of nutrients	**16**	
Calcium, phosphorus and vitamin D	17	
Iron and vitamin C	17	

Current dietary advice

Individuals have varying dietary needs

		✓
Dietary requirements of different groups of individuals	**31**	
Infants	31	
Children	32	
Adolescents	32	
Adults	33	
Elderly People	33	
Dietary requirements of groups with special needs	**34**	
Pregnant women	34	
Lactovegetarians	35	
Vegans	35	
Factors affecting food choice	**36**	
Body size	36	
Age	36	
Gender	36	
Available income	36	
Health	36	
Lifestyle/activities/occupation	37	

Cleanliness is important in relation to health

Safe working practices

		✓
Food preparation	**59**	
Use of sharp knives	59	
Use of gas and electric cookers	59	
Use of electrical equipment	59	
Use of food preparation equipment	60	
Using hot fats, oils and liquids	60	
Care of clothing	**61**	
Use of washing machines	61	
Use of tumble-driers	61	
Use of ironing equipment	61	
Sewing equipment	**62**	
Pins and needles	62	
Scissors	62	
Sewing machines	62	
Home safety	**62**	
Causes and prevention of accidents	62	

Design features

		✓
Influences on choice of materials and resources	**67**	
Food products	70	
Textile items	71	
Conservation of resources	**74**	
Conservation of energy and reduction of running costs	74	
Recycling textiles	78	
Recycling other household products	78	

Physical needs of individuals and families

Management of expenditure

Progression routes and careers

→

Possible careers

The chart below shows some of the possible career routes that can be followed after studying a course in Home Economics. This is by no means a full list but it does give an indication of the wide variety of opportunities available. Further training and study may be required in some areas.

Home Economics Career Areas

Clinical dietician

Clothing buyer/ assistant buyer

Clothing department/ merchandising manager

Clothing education director

Clothing production co-ordinator

Communications: journalist, writer, broadcaster, editor

Community nutrition specialist

Consumer adviser

Consumer relations

Designer

Dietetics: administrator, manager

Dressmaker

Education administration

Family life educator

Fashion: writer, editor, consultant

Food preparer

Food production manager

Food production: development, product testing, marketing, sales, quality assurance

Food/beverage manager

Food/beverage purchasing director

Government family/consumer programs

Home economics teacher

Hotel general manager

Human resources manager

Meat packing company: management, sales

Meat packing quality control supervisor

Meat/food processing: manager

Menu planner

Nutrition: consultant, education

Parent educator

Pattern grader, pattern designer

Pattern maker

Produce supplier

Product development specialist

Product representative: feed, food machinery, chemicals

Product testing and evaluation

Public or private family/child agencies: caseworker, manager

Retail management

Retail manager

Sales/marketing manager

Sports nutrition educator

Store display designer

University professor/ administrator

Progression routes

The chart below shows some possible progression routes that could be followed after studying a Standard Grade course in Home Economics.

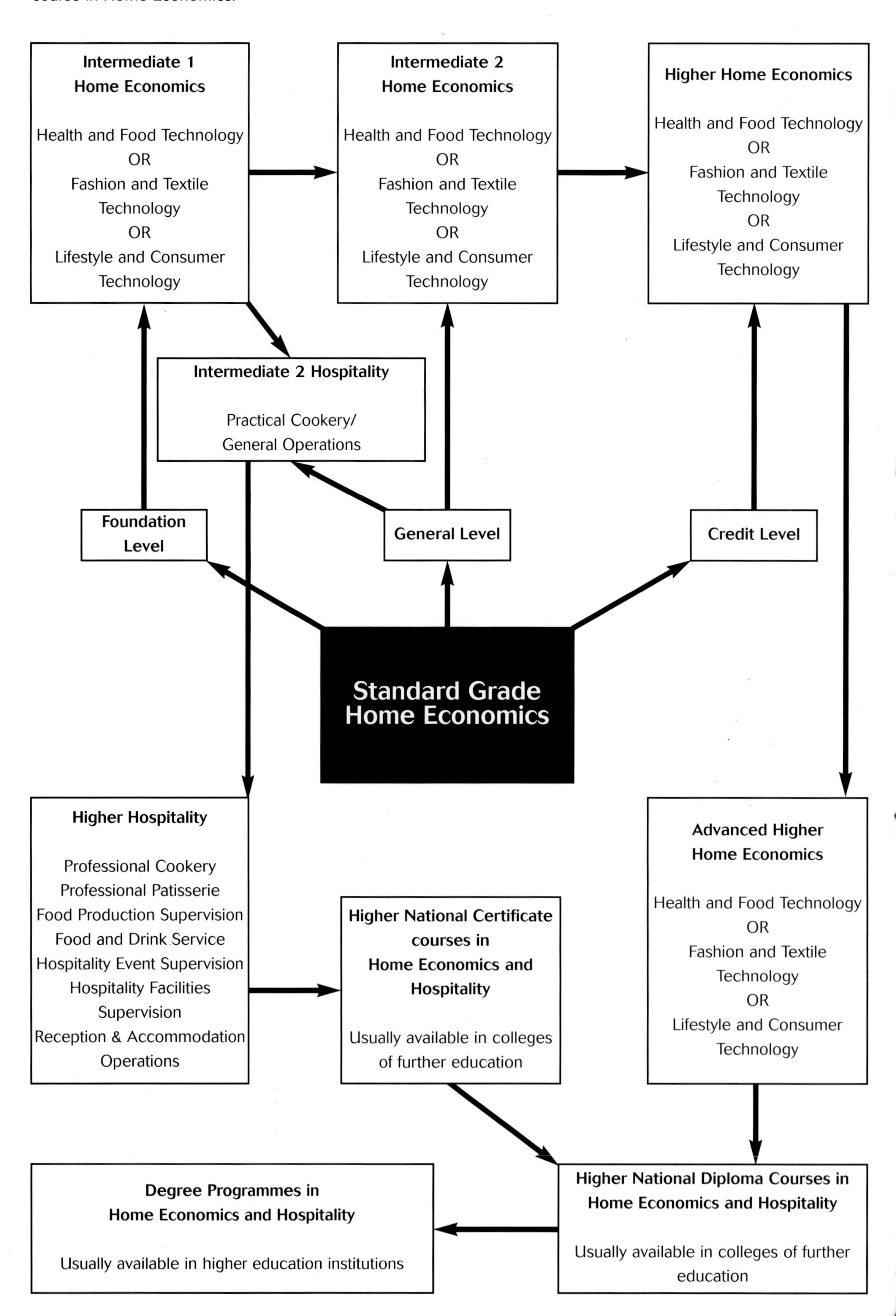